The Need for Alternate Types of Assessment

As the curriculum reforms proposed by Project 2061 of the American Association for the Advancement of Science and by Scope, Sequence, and Coordination of Secondary School Science of the National Science Teachers Association become more and more widely accepted, the need for alternate assessment methods increase. In a fact-driven, concept laden curriculum, using only the traditional paper and pencil testing for knowledge of right answers may be adequate. But the reforms are asking you to assess whether students have gained a deep understanding of the important concepts of science and to assess if they can apply scientific methods in new and novel situations.

How to Use Performance Assessments

Performance Assessments, sometimes referred to as summative assessments, encompass a number of scientific concepts and associated skills. These assessments allow you to analyze the depth of student understanding and give students needed practice in applying concepts and critical thinking.

Each **Performance Assessment** is related to a particular chapter in **SCIENCE INTERACTIONS, COURSE 1.** The **Performance Assessment** allows you to assess student mastery of the chapters concepts as they tackle real-life problems.

How to Use Performance Assessments with SCIENCE INTERACTIONS

After students have completed each text chapter, they then can apply their learning of chapter concepts to the **Performance Assessment** task for that chapter. These activities allow you to assess student mastery as they tackle a real-life problem. They are given a purpose and some ideas about what materials they might use to investigate their problem. The students then must formulate a hypothesis and plan and conduct an investigation. They are then responsible for communicating the results of their investigation and drawing conclusions about their hypothesis and the processes they used.

In order that you might make full use of these performance assessment opportunities, the accompanying Teacher Guide pages identify the processes and concepts that students will spend planning and investigating is indicated. Preparation tips and materials suggestions and alternatives are provided to make purchasing supplies inexpensive and easy. Expected outcome are provided; students may approach the problem in different ways, but there will be important similarities to look for in each investigation. The inclusion of examples of possible student hypotheses and experimental designs helps you be prepared for the questions that are likely to arise. A complete list of materials required for these assessments begins on page vii of this booklet.

Performance Task Assessment Lists and Rubrics found in Glencoe's **Performance Assessment in Middle School Science** can be used by you and your students to assess both the products and processes of the assessment tasks.

Course 1

 This book is printed on recycled paper containing 10% post consumer waste.

GLENCOE
McGraw-Hill

New York, New York   Columbus, Ohio   Mission Hills, California   Peoria, Illinois

A Glencoe Program

Science Interactions

Student Edition

Teacher Wraparound Edition

Science Discovery Activities: SE

Science Discovery Activities: TE

Laboratory Manual: SE

Laboratory Manual: TAE

Study Guide: SE

Study Guide: TE

Transparency Package

Computuer Test Bank

Spanish Resources

Science and Technology Videodisc Series

Science and Technology Videodisc Teacher Guide

Integrated Science Videodisc Program

Send all inquiries to:
Glencoe/McGraw-Hill
936 Eastwind Drive
Westerville, OH 43081

ISBN 0-02-826781-8

Printed in the United States of America.

5 6 7 8 9 10 11 12 BAW 03 02 01 00 99 98 97 96

TABLE OF CONTENTS

Performance Assessments

MATERIALS LIST

The quantities listed are for one class of thirty students working in pairs. Some activities may require larger groups of students due to equipment and space limitations. Materials may be acquired locally or from a commercial supply house.

Nonconsumables

Item	Chapter	Quantity
Apron, laboratory	5, 6	30
Balance, laboratory	7, 11, 14	15
Beaker, large	14	30
Blocks, wood or plastic	17	60
Bones, bird leg, 3 different types	7	15 of each
Bowls, mixing	8	6
Bucket, plastic	6	30
Cardboard, stiff, 25 cm × 90 cm	12	15 pieces
Can opener	4	3
Clipboard	9, 10	15
Clock or timer	3, 8	16
Dowel, wooden, 1-m	19	15
Dropper	5	15
Field Guide	I	2
Funnel	14	30
Gloves, rubber	6	30 pairs
Goggles, safety	6	30 pairs
Graduated cylinder, 100 mL	5, 6, 8, 14	20
Hole punch	13	15
Knife, hobby	4, 10, 12, 13, 16,19	15
Knife, table	11	15
Lamp	2, 19	15
Light bulbs	13	15
Magnifier, hand	7, 10, 11, 14	30
Markers	I, 10	1 set
Measuring cup	4, 5	15
Paper clips	10	1 box
Pencil, with eraser	8	5
Probe	11	30

Nonconsumables

Protractor	19	30
Ruler, customary units	1, 15	15
Ruler, metric	I, 5, 7, 8, 10, 12	15
Scissors	4, 12, 13, 16	15 pairs
Sieves, assorted sizes	11	15 each size
Spoons	8	6
Stirrer	5	15
Stream table	17	15
Test tubes, 22 mm diameter	8	15
Test tube neck	8	5
Thermometer	2, 8	50
Tray	11	30
Tumbler, plastic	5, 6	90
Washers, metal	12	90

Living Organisms

Insects, small crawling	16	15 groups
Plants, small	16	30

Consumables

Adhesive, silicon	13, 16	5 tubes
Bag, plastic garbage	11, 13	70
Bag, plastic resealable	9, 10, 11	60
Ball, styrofoam, 25 cm dia.	19	15
Ball, styrofoam, 6.5 dia.	19	15
Balloons	8	several
Beans, large, dry	4	15 cups
Beans, small, dry	4	15 cups
Bottle, plastic, 16–20 oz., with lids	13, 16	90
Bottle, plastic, 2-L	3, 13, 14	45
Bottle, plastic, 3-L	3, 13	30
Can, coffee	4	60
Clay	16	1 package
Coffee, ground	4	30 cups
Containers, margarine, 48-oz.	4	60

Consumables

Containers, small plastic	16	60
Cornstarch	5	1 box
Egg, chicken	13	3 dozen
Filter paper	14	30 pieces
Glue	12, 19	1 large bottle
Iodine solution	5	1 small bottle
Lid, 48-oz. margarine	4	15
Lid, medicine vial	16	30
Light bulbs, burned out	13	45
Milk carton, half-gallon	13	15
Milk carton, half-pint	13	15
Milk carton, 1-pint	12	8
Newspaper	3	
Orange drink, carbonated	5	1.5 L
Orange drink, 10% juice	5	1.5 L
Orange juice, concentrated	5	3 12-oz. cans
Orange juice, fresh	5	1.5 L
Paper, construction (black, light brown, white)	2	3 sheets each
Paper towels	3, 6, 7, 11, 13	4 rolls
Paper, white	l, 4	16 sheets
Peas, dry	4	15 cups
pH paper	11, 14	2 packages
Push-up disk and stick	12	30 sets
Rice, dry	4	15 cups
Sand	14, 16, 17	1 bag
Screen, nylon	16	4 sq. meters
Skewer	19	30
Soil, potting	14, 16	1 40-lb bag
String, kite	13	1 ball
Stryofoam pieces	3, 13	2 cubic feet
Sugar	8	1 bag
Tape, duct	4	1 roll
Tape, transparent	4, 10, 13, 16	6 rolls
Tubing, plastic	16	30 meters
Yeast, compressed	8	Different brands
Yeast, fast-acting	8	Different brands
Yeast, powdered	8	Different brands

SAFETY IN THE LABORATORY

Following safety procedures in the laboratory is extremely important. Accidents are usually the result of carelessness, not following procedures correctly, or of ignoring warnings. Take lab work seriously. Pay attention to all safety procedures. Here are important safety guidelines to follow when you do laboratory experiments:

SAFETY EQUIPMENT

- Become familiar with the safety equipment available in your laboratory.
- Know where fire extinguishers, fire blankets, safety shower, and first-aid kits are and how to use them. Also, be sure you know where the fire alarm is and where the telephone is, should you need to call for help.

GUARDING YOUR EYES

- Wear goggles or other protective glasses when handling dangerous substances, such as chemicals, or when working with glass equipment. Otherwise, the chemicals or pieces of glass could enter your eyes.
- Should any such substance get into your eyes, wash them immediately with lots of water. Notify your teacher.
- Never use reflected sunlight to illuminate a microscope. Always use a lamp that provides the proper intensity of light needed.

PROTECTING YOUR BODY AND YOUR CLOTHING

- Wear gloves and an apron that covers the front of your clothing when working with chemicals in glassware or over an open flame.
- Tie your hair back so that loose hair cannot catch fire.
- Roll up your sleeves so that they cannot catch fire.
- Never pour water into a strong acid or base solution. The proper procedure is to pour the chemical slowly into the water.
- Never test the smell of a substance by putting your nose directly over the substance. Use your hand to wave the fumes toward you.

USING HEATING EQUIPMENT

- If possible, use a hot plate, not an open flame, to heat substances.
- If you do use an open flame to heat substances in glass containers, use a wire screen with a ceramic center.
- Never point the open end of a heated test tube containing a substance toward yourself or toward anyone else.

PREVENTING INJURIES FROM EQUIPMENT

- Use extreme care when using sharp instruments such as knives, scissors, or nails.
- Be sure that any glass equipment used for heating is heat-resistant. Never use glassware that is cracked or chipped.

CLEANLINESS

- Wash your hands with hot, soapy water after using any dangerous substances.
- Wash all work areas thoroughly. First, be sure to neutralize an acid spill with baking soda or a base spill with boric acid. Then wash the spill area with lots of water.
- Be sure all equipment is clean. Then store the equipment and left-over supplies in the proper place.
- Turn off all running water. Turn off all gas burners or electric plates.

SAFETY SYMBOLS

The *Science Interactions* Program uses safety symbols to alert you to possible laboratory dangers. These symbols are explained below. Be sure you understand each symbol before you begin an activity.

DISPOSAL ALERT
This symbol appears when care must be taken to dispose of materials properly.

ANIMAL SAFETY
This symbol appears whenever live animals are studied and the safety of the animals and the student must be ensured.

BIOLOGICAL HAZARD
This symbol appears when there is danger involving bacteria, fungi, or protists.

RADIOACTIVE SAFETY
This symbol appears when radioactive materials are used.

OPEN FLAME ALERT
This symbol appears when use of an open flame could cause a fire or an explosion.

CLOTHING PROTECTION SAFETY
This symbol appears when substances used could stain or burn clothing.

THERMAL SAFETY
This symbol appears as a reminder to use caution when handling hot objects.

FIRE SAFETY
This symbol appears when care should be taken around open flames.

SHARP OBJECT SAFETY
This symbol appears when a danger of cuts or punctures caused by the use of sharp objects exist.

EXPLOSION SAFETY
This symbol appears when the misuse of chemicals could cause an explosion.

FUME SAFETY
This symbol appears when chemicals or chemical reactions could cause dangerous fumes.

EYE SAFETY
This symbol appears when a danger to the eyes exists. Safety goggles should be worn when this symbol appears.

ELECTRICAL SAFETY
This symbol appears when care should be taken when using electrical equipment.

POISON SAFETY
This symbol appears when poisonous substances are used.

PLANT SAFETY
This symbol appears when poisonous plants or plants with thorns are handled.

CHEMICAL SAFETY
This symbol appears when chemicals used can cause burns or are poisonous if absorbed through the skin.

Choosing Plants to Improve the Soil

Have students complete this performance assessment after they have completed the Introductory chapter of the student text. Students should be allowed to use the textbook and any other reference materials that relate to the study of the Introductory chapter.

PROCESSES AND CONCEPTS
In conducting this investigation, students may use the following processes:

Observing

Inferring

Analyzing data

Using Time/Space Relationships

Constructing Models

Communicating

In conducting this investigation, students may demonstrate knowledge of the following core concepts:

Use of Scientific Methods

Traits of Plants

TIME NEEDED
The time will vary; one to three class periods should be allowed for the planning and investigation.

PREPARATION
Assemble the materials. If possible, have field guides showing photographs or actual samples of the leguminous plants mentioned in the data information sheet for students to examine. You may wish to have a person familiar with reclamation of oil-contaminated soil speak with the class about how soil is cleaned.

SAFETY
No special safety precautions are required.

MONITORING THE INVESTIGATION
Tell the students that you want to review and discuss their plans before they proceed. As each plan is discussed, try to help students recognize flaws in their plans or areas that may require further development. You should not direct their work into any fixed approach. In most performance tasks, there will be different and interesting approaches proposed as solutions. Once plans have been reviewed, have students proceed to the modeling portion of the investigation.

EXPECTED OUTCOMES
This investigation requires students to consider both short-term and long-term solutions to a problem. A logical short-term solution would be to remove the contaminated soil and replace it with either new soil or some type of stone or concrete structure. Short-term solutions for the nitrogen-poor soil will make use of fertilizers.

Long-term solutions to the problem may include having the contaminated soil cleansed and then returned to the area. The use of legumes to enrich the soil is also a long-term solution that will benefit the area by decreasing the likelihood of damage to nearby aquatic ecosystems.

The main goals of this activity are to have students recognize the benefits and drawbacks of their choices and to point out that all solutions to the problem require time to implement. Be sure to check students' reasoning for their selections to see that they have considered the pros and cons of each recommendation.

Going Further Students may suggest that building a playground is an easier way to reclaim the empty lot. For both community projects, the issue of contaminated soil needs to be addressed. Students familiar with oil-consuming microbes may suggest their use as another remedy for soil contamination.

Choosing Plants to Improve
the Soil (continued)

**USING THE PERFORMANCE TASK
ASSESSMENT LIST**
You may use one of the following Performance
Task Assessment Lists: Data Table or Model.

Refer to *Performance Assessment in Middle
School Science* for a discussion of how to use
Performance Task Assessment Lists.

Using Maps to Choose a Location

Have students complete this performance assessment after they have completed Chapter 1 of the student text. Students should be allowed to use the textbook and any other reference materials that relate to the study of Chapter 1.

PROCESSES AND CONCEPTS
In conducting this investigation, students may use the following processes:

Observing
Classifying
Measuring
Using Time/Space
 Relationships

Constructing Models
Identifying Variables
Controlling Variables
Stating Hypotheses
Communicating

In conducting this investigation, students may demonstrate knowledge of the following core concepts:

Identifying landforms
Using latitude and longitude
Effect of landforms
Using physical feature maps
Using topographic maps

TIME NEEDED
The time will vary; one or two class periods should be allowed for the planning and investigation.

PREPARATION
Assemble the materials. Each individual or group should have a set of maps and a textbook.

MONITORING THE INVESTIGATION
Tell the students that you want to review and approve their plan before they proceed. Because the steps in the investigation process are linear and sequential, it will be necessary to make any major corrections before the plan is put into operation.

After the plan is approved, monitor the work of the students, and respond to their questions and procedural requests. You should not direct their work into any fixed approach. In most performance tasks, there will be different and interesting approaches to solutions.

EXPECTED OUTCOMES
This investigation involves using skills to evaluate a manufacturing plant location. This is a task that is undertaken daily in the real world. The students need to read the task statement carefully and identify the variables that need to be considered. In this scenario, such variables might be access to a supply of water or availability of fuel sources. Then they will have to make precise and exact measurements of both vertical and horizontal distances as given by information on the maps. Finally, the longitude and latitude readings and the United States map can be used to look at the problem from a broad basis. While not required, a comparison table will be useful for comparing the sites.

The responses will differ based on both student skills and viewpoints. A sample response might be that site X is more appropriate because of the proximity of large amounts of water. Using the river, lake, rail lines, and highways, raw materials and fuel can easily be shipped in and finished products, out. Even though both cities are likely to have somewhat severe winter weather, the flatness of the land around site X is an advantage to keeping transportation lines open.

Going Further   Other factors to consider may include favorable locations for population growth: nearby undeveloped area for housing, access to centers of commerce, airports within driving distance, etc.

USING THE PERFORMANCE TASK ASSESSMENT LIST
You may use one of the following Performance Task Assessment Lists: Making Observations and Inferences, Carrying Out a Strategy and Collecting Data, or Data Table. Refer to *Performance Assessment in Middle School Science* for a discussion of how to use the Performance Task Assessment Lists.

Choosing Colors

Have students complete this performance assessment after they have completed Chapter 2 of the student text. Students should be allowed to use the textbook and any other reference materials that relate to the study of Chapter 2.

PROCESSES AND CONCEPTS

In conducting this investigation, students may use the following processes:

Observing
Measuring
Inferring
Classifying
Communicating
Using Time/Space Relationships
Identifying Variables
Controlling Variables
Stating Hypotheses

In conducting this investigation, students may demonstrate knowledge of the following core concepts:

Absorption of energy
Properties of light
Impact of light on objects
Definition of light
Definition of color

TIME NEEDED

The time will vary; one to three class periods should be allowed for the planning and investigation.

PREPARATION

Assemble the materials and prepare extra "roof material color" samples. Spend some time setting up light, thermometer, and color-sample systems and observing the effects.

MONITORING THE INVESTIGATION

Tell the students that you want to review and approve their plan before they proceed. Because the steps in the investigation process are linear and sequential, it will be necessary to make any relevant corrections before the plan is put into operation.

After the plan is approved, monitor the work of the students, and respond to their questions and procedural requests. You should not direct their work into any fixed approach. In most performance tasks, there will be different and interesting approaches to solutions.

EXPECTED OUTCOMES

Colored objects have different properties, and this investigation looks at the relationship of color to reflection and absorption of energy from light. In general, the darker color will reflect less and absorb more energy. Some students may investigate other variables. For example, the effect of the angle of incidence can be found by adjusting the angle at which the light strikes the roofing material. Students will find that the more direct the rays are as they strike the surface, the more energy is absorbed. The Evaluation Form will allow you to monitor student work for consistency.

Going Further Other factors to consider may include the aesthetic qualities and the price of the materials involved.

USING THE PERFORMANCE TASK ASSESSMENT LIST

You may use one of the following Performance Task Assessment Lists: Model, Data Table, or Graph from Data. Refer to *Performance Assessment in Middle School Science* for a discussion of how to use Performance Task Assessment Lists.

Quieter Cars

Have students complete this performance assessment after they have completed Chapter 3 of the student text. Students should be allowed to use the textbook and any other reference materials that relate to the study of Chapter 3.

PROCESSES AND CONCEPTS

In conducting this investigation, students may use the following processes:

Observing
Measuring
Using Time/Space
    Relationships
Making Operational
    Definitions
Communicating

Constructing Models
Identifying Variables
Controlling Variables
Stating Hypotheses

In conducting this investigation, students may demonstrate knowledge of the following core concepts:

Frequency of sound
Production of sound
Properties of sound

Sources of sound
Travel of sound
    through matter

TIME NEEDED

The time will vary; one to three class periods should be allowed for the planning and investigation.

PREPARATION

Assemble the materials. You will need to prepare the two plastic drink container sections. Both of the domed sections must fit over and cover the timer or clock (sound source). After preparing the plastic domes, set up an insulation system and observe the effects.

MONITORING THE INVESTIGATION

Tell the students that you want to review and approve their plan before they proceed. Because the steps in the investigation process are linear and sequential, it will be necessary to make any relevant corrections before the plan is put into operation.

After the plan is approved, monitor the work of the students, and respond to their questions and procedural requests. You should not direct their work into any fixed approach. In most performance tasks, there will be different and interesting approaches to solutions.

EXPECTED OUTCOMES

This investigation examines the way sound is absorbed when it travels through matter. With two containers and a variety of insulating materials, there can be some interesting designs. A common design utilizes one dome inside the other with insulation material placed between the two domes. Sound-measuring meters can be purchased from many electronics stores. If sound-measuring equipment is not available, the students must come up with some method for agreeing on sound levels. You may want them to demonstrate this process for you.

Going Further   Other factors to consider may include safety, durability, aesthetic qualities, and cost of these new noise reduction designs.

USING THE PERFORMANCE TASK ASSESSMENT LIST

You may use one of the following Performance Task Assessment Lists: Making Observations and Inferences, Data Table, or Graph from Data. Refer to *Performance Assessment in Middle School Science* for a discussion of how to use Performance Task Assessment Lists.

Have students complete this performance assessment after they have completed Chapter 4 of the student text. Students should be allowed to use the textbook and any other reference materials that relate to the study of Chapter 4.

PROCESSES AND CONCEPTS
In conducting this investigation, students may use the following processes:

Observing	Using Time/Space
Classifying	Relationships
Measuring	Identifying Variables
Communicating	Controlling Variables
Building Models	Stating Hypotheses

In conducting this investigation, students may demonstrate knowledge of the following concepts:

Physical properties	Identifying mixtures
of matter	Separating mixtures
Properties of solids	Using the metric system

TIME NEEDED
The time will vary; one to three class periods should be allowed for the planning and investigation.

PREPARATION
Assemble the materials. You may prefer to remove the bottoms of three of the four margarine tubs or coffee cans rather than have students do this. If students remove these themselves, caution them that the knife and the edges where the can was cut are sharp, and caution should be observed.

MONITORING THE INVESTIGATION
Tell the students that you want to review and approve their plan before they proceed. Because the steps in the investigation process are linear and sequential, it will be necessary to make any major corrections before the plan is put into operation.

After the plan is approved, monitor the work of the students, and respond to their questions and procedural requests. You should not direct their work into any fixed approach. In most performance tasks, there will be different and interesting approaches to solutions.

EXPECTED OUTCOMES
This investigation involves designing and building a set of sieves capable of sorting three useful materials and the nonuseful material that contains them. A model of this mixture is made by using rice, coffee, and two sizes of beans. There are several ways to set up the sieve system. Meshes of different sizes can be made by using paper strips with different-sized holes between them or by using pieces of paper with different-sized holes cut in them. The most efficient system will probably be some type of stack system with the largest mesh separating the top two tubs or cans and a tub or can with its bottom intact at the bottom. This system should sort the 5-cup mixture rapidly and efficiently. For the timed experiment, it is not necessary to sort the entire 5-cup mixture by hand. A 1-cup mixture can be used for the timed experiment.

Going Further   Other factors that are important may include the ability to upscale the model to a production level, the cost involved, and whether the raw materials to be separated could be damaged during the process.

USING THE PERFORMANCE TASK ASSESSMENT LIST
You may use one of the following Performance Task Assessment Lists: Invention, Data Table, or Graph from Data. Refer to *Performance Assessment in Middle School Science* for a discussion of how to use Performance Task Assessment Lists.

Reaching High C

Have students complete this performance assessment after they have completed Chapter 5 of the student text. Students should be allowed to use the textbook and any other reference materials that relate to the study of Chapter 5.

PROCESSES AND CONCEPTS

In conducting this investigation, students may use the following processes:

Observing	Identifying Variables
Measuring	Stating Hypotheses
Inferring	Predicting
Classifying	Controlling Variables
Communicating	

In conducting this investigation, students may demonstrate knowledge of the following core concepts:

Definition of solution	Concentration of solutions
Definition of solubility	
Definition of solute	Definition of solvent

TIME NEEDED

The time will vary; one to three class periods should be allowed for the planning and investigation.

PREPARATION

Assemble the materials. You can either prepare and test the iodine-starch indicator solution or you can have the students prepare and test it. To prepare the indicator solution, place about 6 g of cornstarch in 250 mL of cool water in a heat-proof container. Place this container on a heat source, and stir the solution while bringing it to a boil. Boil for two minutes. Add ten droppersful of this solution to one gallon of water. (A clean gallon milk jug will work well for mixing and storing this solution.) Add one dropperful of iodine solution to the gallon of starch solution, and mix well. The solution should turn blue. This is the indicator solution that the students will use to test for vitamin C.

In performing this test, students have to assume that all vitamin C present comes from orange juice and that no additional vitamin C has been added by the manufacturer.

You may want to have other foods available for those students who would like to check the vitamin C content. Fruits such as grapes and kiwi work well.

SAFETY

As with any unknown solution, warn the students not to taste any of the materials. Iodine solution is toxic and will stain clothes and skin. Laboratory aprons should be worn. If preparing their own indicator solution, goggles should also be worn by students.

MONITORING THE INVESTIGATION

Tell the students you want to review and approve their plan before they proceed. Allow them to experiment with the indicator solution and orange juice until they can establish an experimental baseline, which they can use as a standard for comparison. This should be done before the plan is completed. Because the steps in the plan are sequential, it will be necessary to make any major corrections before the plan is put into operation.

After the plan is approved, monitor the work of the students, and respond to their questions and procedural requests. The establishment of baseline data is necessary. You should not, however, direct student work into any fixed approach. In most performance tasks, there will be different and interesting approaches to solutions.

EXPECTED OUTCOMES

This investigation examines the relative quantities of vitamin C, an essential requirement for good health, in various orange drinks. A procedure that works well is to pour the indicator to a depth of 1 cm in the tumblers. The drink being tested can be added drop by drop to the indicator. Stir between each addition. The establishment of a baseline for color change in the indicator solution is critical. The amount of fresh orange juice required to change the color of the indicator is a common baseline. Any of the solutions with the exception of the carbonated drink can be used to establish the baseline, however, and this will affect the procedure. Exact measurement is also critical.

Results will vary greatly depending on the products chosen. In general, students will find that orange juice from freshly squeezed oranges and from concentrate are similar in vitamin C content and have the most vitamin C. The 10 percent drink will have a measurable amount, but most carbonated orange drinks have little, if any, vitamin C.

Going Further You must assume that all vitamin C present comes from the orange juice itself and that no additional vitamin C has been added by the manufacturer. This may not be a reasonable assumption. Vitamins and other nutrients are often added to food products.

USING THE PERFORMANCE TASK ASSESSMENT LIST
You may use one of the following Performance Task Assessment Lists: Designing an Experiment, Data Table, or Graph from Data. Refer to *Performance Assessment in Middle School Science* for a discussion of how to use Performance Task Assessment Lists.

Acids and Bases in Your Home

Have students complete this performance assessment after they have completed Chapter 6 of the student text. Students should be allowed to use the textbook and any other reference materials that relate to the study of Chapter 6.

PROCESSES AND CONCEPTS
In conducting this investigation, students may use the following processes:

Observing	Identifying Variables
Measuring	Controlling Variables
Classifying	Communicating

In conducting this investigation, students may demonstrate knowledge of the following core concepts:

Properties of acids	Identifying bases
Identifying acids	pH indicators
Acid-base indicators	pH scale
Properties of bases	

TIME NEEDED
The time will vary; one or two class periods should be allowed for the planning and investigation.

PREPARATION
Assemble the materials. You should be able to locate most of them at the grocery store. If you cannot locate an environmentally safe cleaner, you can mix vinegar, lemon juice, salt, and witch hazel or an aromatic flavoring. To order environmentally safe cleaners call 1-800-328-4408. Mix up a set of the test products and test them with broad range pH paper. Record your results for reference. This will allow you to assist the students in their investigation.

Oven cleaners (base), toilet bowl cleaners (acid), and automatic dishwashing detergent (base) will give very definite results that will be in the extremes of the pH range. They may, however, be too reactive for students this age to use safely. You may choose to test them as a demonstration.

SAFETY
Tell students to wear rubber gloves, goggles, and aprons when mixing and handling solutions.

MONITORING THE INVESTIGATION
Tell the students that you want to review and approve their plan before they proceed. Allow them to experiment with the pH paper and known solutions such as tap water (neutral), cola drink (acid), and baking soda (base) until they can read and interpret the pH scale. This should be done before the plan is written. Because the steps in the plan are sequential, it will be necessary to make any major corrections before the plan is put into operation.

After the plan is approved, monitor the work of the students and respond to their questions and procedural requests. You should not direct their work into any fixed approach. In most performance tasks, there will be different and interesting approaches to solutions.

EXPECTED OUTCOMES
This investigation uses a universal pH indicator to assign numerical values to various household cleaners, soaps, and shampoos. Some interesting results will emerge depending on what materials are placed in the set of test materials. If you can find a wide range of products, you will see a wide range of pH values. In general, the traditional household cleaners will be strong bases. Most shampoos are neutral or, as the advertisement used to say, "pH balanced." The soaps will show a range from neutral to basic. On the other hand, the environmentally safe cleaners will be neutral to strongly acidic. The similarity of the shampoos introduces students to the common phenomena of "no significant difference." Allow students to use the labels of the test products to assist them in drawing meaningful conclusions.

Going Further Other factors to consider may include side effects of the product (household cleaners and soaps may be too strong for sensitive/young skin), odor and appearance may be offensive, cost may be excessive.

Acids and Bases in Your Home (continued)

USING THE PERFORMANCE TASK ASSESSMENT LIST

You may use one of the following Performance Task Assessment Lists: Data Table or Graph from Data. Refer to *Performance Assessment in Middle School Science* for a discussion of how to use Performance Task Assessment Lists.

Birds of a Feather?

Have students complete this performance assessment after they have completed Chapter 7 of the student text. Students should be allowed to use the textbook and any other reference materials that relate to the study of Chapter 7.

PROCESS AND CONCEPTS

In conducting this investigation, students may use the following processes:

Observing	Constructing Models
Measuring	Identifying Variables
Inferring	Communicating
Classifying	

In conducting this investigation, students may demonstrate knowledge of the following core concepts:

Characteristics of living things	Relationships of organisms
Classification systems	Traits used to classify organisms
Levels of classification systems	

TIME NEEDED

The time will vary; one to three class periods should be allowed for the planning and investigation.

PREPARATION

Assemble the materials. The key to this investigation is the variety of bird leg bones. The local supermarket or poultry distributor will have a selection of fresh and frozen carcasses. Just the legs can be purchased for some birds. You can select from:

fryer chickens	roasting ducks
roasting chickens	game hens
small turkeys	roasting geese
large turkeys	

If there are hunters and game farms in the area, you may be able to acquire dove, quail, wild geese, pheasant, wild ducks, and grouse.

Select three poultry legs. An interesting and readily available selection would be a small fryer (two pounds dressed weight), a domestic duck (4–6 pounds), and a small turkey (8–10 pounds). Boil each leg until the flesh can be easily removed. The meat and stock can be used for soups and in other recipes. Cool and rinse the legs. Use a stiff brush to remove any remaining connective tissue and dry thoroughly. To add a realistic look to the bones and sanitize them, soak them for 30 minutes in a mixture of 1 part household bleach and 2 parts water. Then place the bones in bags labeled A, B, and C.

Going Further Fish skeletons are usually very easily removed from whole, cooked fish. Bone kits are also available from scientific supply houses. Use Expected Outcomes for reference.

MONITORING THE INVESTIGATION

Tell the students that you want to review and approve their plan before they proceed. Because the steps in the investigation process are linear and sequential, it will be necessary to make any relevant corrections before the plan is put into operation.

After the plan is approved, monitor the work of the students, and respond to their questions and procedural requests. You should not direct their work into any fixed approach. In most performance tasks, there will be different and interesting approaches to solutions.

EXPECTED OUTCOMES

This investigation uses classification skills to identify similarities and differences in leg bones from three different birds. The results and identification will depend on the specific birds chosen for the investigation. Significant variables will include bone length, density, structure, and overall shape. If turkey, duck, and chicken bones are chosen, significant differences can be seen in density and length. Birds that fly or swim more than walk, such as a duck, will have leg bones that are shorter and less dense than

Birds of a Feather? (continued)

the legs of a bird such as a turkey, which primarily bears its weight on its legs. Because of its weight and the fact that it primarily walks, turkey legs are more dense, have additional small bones, and have dense bone where other birds may have cartilage. Leg bones for closely related birds such as chickens and game hens are very similar, differing only in size.

USING THE PERFORMANCE TASK ASSESSMENT LIST

You may use one of the following Performance Task Assessment Lists: Making and Using a Classification System or Data Table. Refer to *Performance Assessment in Middle School Science* for a discussion of how to use Performance Task Assessment Lists.

Rising Expectations

Have students complete this performance assessment after they have completed Chapter 8 of the student text. Students should be allowed to use the textbook and any other reference materials that relate to the study of Chapter 8.

PROCESSES AND CONCEPTS
In conducting this investigation, students may use the following processes:

Observing
Measuring
Organizing and Analyzing Data
Identifying Variables
Controlling Variables
Communicating
Inferring

In conducting this investigation, students may demonstrate knowledge of the following core concepts:

Cellular respiration
Characteristics of living organisms

TIME NEEDED
Two or three class periods. Allow one class period to observe the interaction between the yeast and the sugar-water solution, and its effect on the balloon. A second class period can be used to design the investigation and carry out the comparison of the effectiveness of different yeast products. A third class period may be necessary to write the summary.

PREPARATION
Supply spoons, metric ruler, graduated cylinder, mixing bowl(s), wax marking pencil, white table sugar, thermometers, balloons, and test tubes in racks. Several brands and forms of yeast should be available.

Locate a place for students to store their solutions, so that students can monitor their experiments over a 24- or 48-hour period.

SAFETY
To protect their clothing, students should wear laboratory aprons throughout this investigation.

MONITORING THE INVESTIGATION
Controlling variables is a key to reliable results in this experiment. Watch to see if students design their experiments using two or three brands of just one form only. This will reduce the number of variables and make drawing conclusions much easier. If students begin to manipulate too many variables (a variety of brands and forms) they may become confused. Students should also discover that the amount of water, sugar, and yeast should be constant in all tests. Water temperature must be controlled according to the package directions for each yeast product. Each yeast solution should be evaluated in at least two trials. Once samples are prepared, test tubes in racks should be placed in a warm place away from drafts.

Some students may have difficulty managing their time. Set time checkpoints on the chalkboard and encourage students to keep track of their time using the checkpoints as a model.

EXPECTED OUTCOMES
Each student or group should have his or her own plan for evaluating the different yeast products. The plan should include a strategy for measuring the relative effectiveness of the yeast by comparing the inflation of the balloons. Measurements could be taken across the diameter of each balloon at timed intervals.

Each student will write a summary of his or her experiment and reach a conclusion about which yeast produced the best results. The summary should describe in general what takes place when yeast utilizes sugar as a source of energy. The summary should also explain why the ballon inflates.

Going Further   This performance assessment provides an excellent opportunity to review the importance of controlling variables during an experiment. A discussion of sources of experimental error should take place.

The design of the bread dough experiments will vary, but the amounts of flour, sugar, yeast, and water should be constant for all tests a student runs. A measured amount of each dough sample should be placed in a container, such as a test tube or a 25-ml graduated cylinder. The volume of each dough sample should be measured at regular intervals. The increase in volume of each dough sample can be used as a measure of the effectiveness of the yeast.

Another test of the yeast would be to actually make and bake bread. Students can work at home or with the home economics teacher to carry out the activity.

USING THE PERFORMANCE TASK ASSESSMENT LIST
You may use one of the following Performance Task Assessment Lists: Making Observations and Inferences, Designing an Experiment, Carrying Out a Strategy and Collecting Data, or Data Table. Refer to *Performance Assessment in Middle School Science* for a discussion on how to use Performance Task Assessment Lists.

Adaptations for Survival

Have students complete this performance assessment after they have completed Chapter 9 of the student text. Students should be allowed to use the textbook and any other reference materials that relate to the study of Chapter 9.

PROCESSES AND CONCEPTS
In conducting this investigation, students may use the following processes:

Observing	Communicating
Measuring	Using Time/Space Relation-
Inferring	ship
Predicting	Identifying Variable
Classifying	

In conducting this investigation, students may demonstrate knowledge of the following core concepts:

Adaptation in animals	Behavior of animals
Adaptation and survival	Characteristics of animals

TIME NEEDED
The time will vary; allow one or two class periods for the planning and investigation.

PREPARATION
Assemble the materials. This is a simulation, and you will need the following additional materials to represent the two organisms.

Toothpickus brightus
20 yellow toothpicks
(Regular toothpicks can be dyed with yellow and green food coloring.)

Toothpickus dullus
100 green toothpicks

Locate a small open grassy area that has been mowed. A school yard lawn will be adequate. Mark off a square area and randomly distribute the colored toothpicks by sprinkling them. The survey area should be approximately 8 to 10 meters square. You can mark it with stakes and string if you want to. If weather is not permitting or grass is not available, a large section of artificial grass can be used with a reduced number of toothpicks.

MONITORING THE INVESTIGATION
Discuss the Species Identification material with students before they plan their investigations. Tell the students that you want to review and approve their plan before they proceed.

After the plan is approved, monitor the work of the students and respond to their questions and procedural requests. You should not direct their work into any fixed approach. In most performance tasks, there will be different and interesting approaches to solutions.

EXPECTED OUTCOMES
The two organisms are identical except in color. The baseline population was 40 for one species and 50 for the second species. The current population is 20 for the first species and 100 for the second. Given enough time (up to one hour) students should be able to locate 80 to 90% of both species. However, due to the adaptation of protective coloration, the green species should be more difficult to locate. (Note: if you are doing this in late fall or winter and the grass is dead and yellow, reverse the numbers of the colored toothpicks. The key is to distribute the larger number of the organism that has benefitted from protective coloration.) The student reports should reflect protective coloration as the adaptation that has contributed to lessened predation and increased populations through reproduction.

The Assessment Task Evaluation Form that precedes this chapter-by-chapter teaching material gives you an outline for evaluating student outcomes.

Going Further Different seasons produce different ground covering. In the late spring and summer, the ground may be covered with grass, while in autumn, the ground could be covered with colorful, fallen leaves. Therefore due to camouflaging effects, the green toothpicks may be difficult to find in summer and the yellow toothpicks may be difficult to find in autumn.

Surveying Seed Plants

Have students complete this performance assessment after they have completed Chapter 10 in the student text. Students should be allowed to use the textbook and any other reference materials that relate to the study of Chapter 10.

PROCESSES AND CONCEPTS
In conducting this investigation, students may use the following processes:

Observing
Inferring
Using Time/Space
   Relationships

Constructing Models
Identifying Variables
Communicating

In conducting this investigation, students may demonstrate knowledge of the following core concepts:

Traits of plants
Plant structures
Vascular plants
Angiosperms

Gymnosperms
Monocots
Dicots

TIME NEEDED
The time will vary; one to three class periods should be allowed for the planning and investigation.

PREPARATION
Assemble the materials. If it is not possible to conduct a field survey in your area, assemble a selection of seed plants that are typical of your area and can be brought into the classroom. If you are able to conduct the survey on school grounds or in the local area, inspect the area thoroughly and conduct a preliminary survey.

SAFETY
The field investigation requires monitoring. The study area should be clearly defined or mapped, and, if needed, volunteer monitors should be used. A thorough safety briefing should be completed before the field survey begins to warn students about any poisonous or otherwise harmful plants or animals in your area.

MONITORING THE INVESTIGATION
Tell the students that you want to review and approve their plan before they proceed. Because the steps in the investigation process are linear and sequential, it will be necessary to make any relevant corrections before the plan is put into operation.

After the plan is approved, monitor the work of the students, and respond to their questions and procedural requests. You should not direct their work into any fixed approach. In most performance tasks, there will be different and interesting approaches to solutions.

EXPECTED OUTCOMES
This investigation uses botanical survey techniques to locate and identify seed plants in a study area. The students are directed to develop a survey form, such as the following form, based on an information sheet. The form should include classification categories for gymnosperms, angiosperms, and subcategories for monocots and dicots. It should also describe a checklist for descriptional characteristics such as leaves, stems, seeds, and flowers. If nonvascular and seedless vascular plants are in the area, a category could exist to list them. Students should place each plant in its own category, but should rely on the description, not the name, of the plant for identification.

Category	Sample	General Observations	Meets the category's description for:			
			leaves	stems	seeds	flowers
Gymnosperms	1	Large tree found by the northwest corner of the school; a conifer	✓	✓	✓	✓
	2	Shrub to the left of the front door of the school	✓	✓	✓	✓
Angiosperms: Monocots	1	Wheat growing in field	✓	✓	✓	Not observed

Going Further Other factors to consider may include climate, location (surburban or urban), pollution sources (nearby factories, automobiles), etc.

USING THE PERFORMANCE TASK ASSESSMENT LIST

You may use one of the following Performance Task Assessment Lists: Making and Using a Classification System or Data Table. Refer to *Performance Assessment in Middle School Science* for a discussion of how to use Performance Task Assessment Lists.

It's Dirty Work

Have students complete this performance assessment after they have completed Chapter 11 of the student text. Students should be allowed to use the textbook and any other reference materials that relate to the study of Chapter 11.

PROCESS AND CONCEPTS
In conducting this investigation, students may use the following processes:

Observing
Measuring
Classifying
Identifying Variables
Using Time/Space Relationships
Communicating

In conducting this investigation, students may demonstrate knowledge of the following core concepts:

Formation of soil
Examining soil
Materials in soil
Traits of soil
Types of soil
Soil profiles

TIME NEEDED
The time will vary; one or two class periods should be allowed for the planning and investigation. For greatest time efficiency, students will need to immediately start the drying process needed to determine moisture content, and then do other planning and observing while the sample dries.

PREPARATION
Assemble the materials. You can collect the soil samples or you can supervise the students as they collect them. If you have a soil core sampler, you can use it to obtain two soil columns from the same area. If you do not have a core sampler, you can use a narrow spade or trowel to obtain a column, then cut the column in half vertically. Place the two samples in pans or trays on a plastic sheet.

When the planning phase begins, point out to students that an oven is available to evaporate moisture from the samples. To remove the moisture from the soil, set an oven on low heat (200° F) and heat the sample 4 to 8 hours. If an oven is not available, try to arrange an alternate drying method, such as placing the sample in a sunny, dry location with good air flow.

SAFETY
Warn students to be very careful when using sharp objects. You may want to supervise the use of cutting instruments, if used.

MONITORING THE INVESTIGATION
Tell the students that you want to review and approve their plan before they proceed. Because the steps in the investigation process are linear and sequential, it will be necessary to make any relevant corrections before the plan is put into operation.

After the plan is approved, monitor the work of the students, and respond to their questions and procedural requests. You should not direct their work into any fixed approach. In most performance tasks, there will be different and interesting approaches to solutions.

EXPECTED OUTCOMES
This investigation uses both nondestructive and destructive procedures to analyze a soil sample. While approaches will differ, students should observe the nondestroyed sample with hand magnifiers and probes. A small amount can be removed for pH testing. The sample can be observed with a hand magnifier to see if any animal life is present. The plant material can be observed, and any interesting characteristics can be noted.

After you inform the students that an oven is available to evaporate the moisture from the other sample, they should develop a process for determining moisture content. After the sample is heated and reweighed, it can be crushed, sifted, and observed. The six categories mentioned in The Problem should be treated in the student report.

Going Further Other factors to consider may include the amount of organic material present or the porosity of the soil. Other considerations might be what minerals are present in the soil and how well plants grow in it.

USING THE PERFORMANCE TASK ASSESSMENT LIST
You may use one of the following Performance Task Assessment Lists: Making Observations and Inferences, Data Table, or Analyzing the Data. Refer to *Performance Assessment in Middle School Science* for a discussion of how to use Performance Task Assessment Lists.

Teacher Guides

Maximum Motion

Have students complete this performance assessment after they have completed Chapter 12 of the student text. Students should be allowed to use the textbook and any other reference materials that relate to the study of Chapter 12.

PROCESSES AND CONCEPTS

In conducting this investigation, students may use the following processes:

Observing	Constructing Models
Measuring	Identifying Variables
Inferring	Controlling Variables
Predicting	Stating Hypotheses
Using Time/Space Relationships	Communicating

In conducting this investigation, students may demonstrate knowledge of the following core concepts:

Acceleration due to gravity	Velocity along a straight line
Motion and position	Measuring distance
Speed and distance	

TIME NEEDED

The time will vary; one to three class periods should be allowed for the planning and investigation.

PREPARATION

Assemble the materials. You can use a hobby knife or scissors to cut the milk cartons in half, top to bottom, making a perpendicular cut across the top closure. You may choose to let the students do the cutting. The wheels and axles are found in ice cream novelties known as "push ups." These novelties are found in most supermarkets. Be sure the straws have a large enough diameter that the "push up" sticks will turn easily when placed in the straws. You may want to build a model and try it. Start with full-width wheels. The discs can be trimmed, forming narrower wheels to decrease friction.

An option would be to use a Cub Scout "Pinewood Derby" race car kit.

SAFETY

This investigation requires the use of knives and scissors. Warn students to be careful. You may want to supervise use of cutting instruments.

MONITORING THE INVESTIGATION

Tell the students that you want to review and approve their plan before they proceed. Because the steps in the investigation process are linear and sequential, it will be necessary to make any major corrections before the plan is put into operation.

After the plan is approved, monitor the work of the students, and respond to their questions and procedural requests. You should not direct their work into any fixed approach. In most performance tasks, there will be different and interesting approaches to solutions.

EXPECTED OUTCOMES

This investigation involves many of the variables that affect linear motion in wheeled vehicles. The most significant variable is friction. Reducing friction involves such tasks as trimming wheel width and hubs and removing material that interferes with the rotation of axles. Weight of the gravity-driven vehicle is also important.

Several designs can emerge. In common designs, drinking straws are passed through holes in the body (one-half of the milk carton) or glued on the bottom of the body. Axles then turn inside the straws. Students may reduce air resistance by making modifications such as cutting out the back of the car (bottom of the milk carton). Some designs will use the carton open-side-up, others will use the carton open-side-down.

Going Further The materials or features that might be suggested in the Going Further section include those that reduce air resistance or friction in the wheel assembly. Students might suggest additions that would result in a less "boxy" design for the body. Other materials such as stiffer plastic, metal rods, and wooden or rubber wheels could be considered in addition to more aerodynamic features.

USING THE PERFORMANCE TASK ASSESSMENT LIST
Use the Performance Task Assessment List for Model. Refer to *Performance Assessment in Middle School Science* for a discussion of how to use Performance Task Assessment Lists.

Teacher Guides

Safe Landings

Have students complete this performance assessment after they have completed Chapter 13 of the student text. Students should be allowed to use the textbook and any other reference materials that relate to the study of Chapter 13.

PROCESSES AND CONCEPTS

In conducting this investigation, students may use the following processes:

Observing
Measuring
Communicating
Constructing Models
Controlling Variables

Using Time/Space Relationships
Making Operational Definitions
Identifying Variables

In conducting this investigation, students may demonstrate knowledge of the following core concepts:

Acceleration of falling objects
Acceleration due to gravity

Terminal velocity
Motion of falling bodies

TIME NEEDED

The time will vary; one to three class periods should be allowed for the planning and investigation. Special time arrangements may be necessary for the final system test.

PREPARATION

Assemble the materials. The plastic squares can be cut out of plastic garbage bags. You can cut out hexagonal parachutes from the plastic or you can leave this for the students. See the diagram for a sample parachute construction and basic system design. Locate a suitable drop site. If necessary, adjust the 10-m drop height to the height of your location. The top of a school building, an upper floor of a multistory building, or the top row of a football stadium will provide challenging locations. You will need assistance in monitoring for safety, and you may want to test several designs at one time. Weather conditions are also important, and wind speeds should be less than 5 miles per hour.

Discuss with students what a *payload* is, and how these items that deal with the purpose of a mission differ from the items that are necessary for the operation of the mission vehicle.

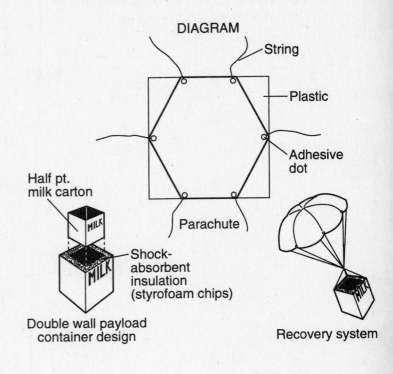

DIAGRAM

String

Plastic

Adhesive dot

Half pt. milk carton

Parachute

Shock-absorbent insulation (styrofoam chips)

Double wall payload container design

Recovery system

SAFETY

This investigation involves the use of knives and scissors. You should caution the students and monitor their use of the cutting instruments. Be sure an adequate number of monitors are present for the testing and a safe site is chosen.

MONITORING THE INVESTIGATION

Tell the students that you want to review and approve their plan before they proceed. Allow them to do limited testing of their recovery system using old light bulbs. This is a complex problem. Because the steps in the investigation process are linear and sequential, it will be necessary to make any major corrections before the plan is put into operation.

After the plan is approved, monitor the work of the students and respond to their questions and procedural requests. You should not direct their work into any fixed approach. In most perfor-

Safe Landings (continued)

mance tasks, there will be different and interesting approaches to solutions.

EXPECTED OUTCOMES

This investigation looks at the problem of delivering an object safely to a planet surface and involves using a combination of devices to accomplish this. NASA and other organizations use a combination of parachutes and collapsible or crushable containers with internal padding. With the variety of materials, your students will produce an interesting array of designs. A sample system is shown in the diagram.

Going Further The moon has approximately one-sixth the gravitational pull of Earth. A payload dropped toward the surface of the moon would have a much "softer" fall. A payload delivery system on the moon would, however, have to have shock-absorbing features. There would be no atmosphere and thus no air resistance, so a parachute assembly would not be effective.

USING THE PERFORMANCE TASK ASSESSMENT LIST

You may use one of the following Performance Task Assessment Lists: Data Table or Model. Refer to *Performance Assessment in Middle School Science* for a discussion of how to use Performance Task Assessment Lists.

Well, Well, Well

Have students complete this performance assessment after they have completed Chapter 14 of the student text. Students should be allowed to use the textbook and any other reference materials that relate to the study of Chapter 14.

PROCESSES AND CONCEPTS

In conducting this investigation, students may use the following processes:

Observing	Constructing Models
Measuring	Identifying Variables
Inferring	Controlling Variables
Predicting	Communicating

In conducting this investigation, students may demonstrate knowledge of the following core concepts:

Processes in the hydrologic cycle
Land slope and stream formation
Soil porosity and permeability
Groundwater, aquifers, and the water table

TIME NEEDED

The time will vary; one or two class periods should be allowed for the planning and investigation.

PREPARATION

Assemble the materials. The diagram shows how to construct the soil-rock column models. These column models will allow you to pour water in the top and collect water at the bottom. These water samples would represent the quality of water that would end up in the proposed city water supply. You can vary the amounts, type, depth, and sequence of soil, sand, pebbles, and rocks that you place in the model. Experiment with several different models and examine the effluent for clarity and contents.

Soil-Rock Column Models

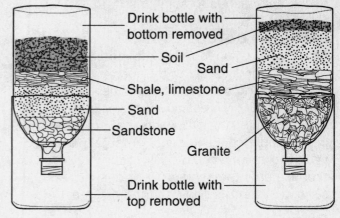

Drink bottle with bottom removed
Soil
Sand
Shale, limestone
Sand
Sandstone
Granite
Drink bottle with top removed

MONITORING THE INVESTIGATION

Tell the students that you want to review and approve their plan before they proceed. Allow them to experiment with the pH paper and various solutions (tap water, vinegar, baking soda, for example) as a reminder of how to read and interpret the pH scale. This should be done before the plan is written. Because the steps in the plan are sequential, it will be necessary to make any major corrections before the plan is put into operation.

After the plan is approved, monitor the work of the students, and respond to their questions and procedural requests. You should not direct their work into any fixed approach. In most performance tasks, there will be different and interesting approaches to solutions.

EXPECTED OUTCOMES

This investigation uses models of two different soil-rock combinations that exist in a community's proposed new water supply areas. According to how the column models are structured, there will be differences in the clarity and color of the water emerging from the columns and possibly the pH of the water. Students should use the equipment to analyze the water from the column models.

The time of flow through the column into the catch basin is also of interest. In general, the longer the time of flow, the more the water is filtered, and the clarity increases. The number of trials through the model will also affect the results. As the number of trials increases, much of the soluble material and many of the loose particles will be removed, and water clarity should increase. Based on these factors, students should be able to organize the data and reach a conclusion.

Going Further   Other factors to consider may include proximity of water source to the city it is supplying, and the proximity of potential pollution sources such as industry and agriculture.

USING THE PERFORMANCE TASK ASSESSMENT LIST

You may use one of the following Performance Task Assessment Lists: Carrying Out a Strategy and Collecting Data, Analyzing the Data, Model, or Data Table. Refer to *Performance Assessment in Middle School Science* for a discussion of how to use Performance Task Assessment Lists.

Down in the Valley

Have students complete this performance assessment after they have completed Chapter 15 of the student text. Students should be allowed to use the textbook and any other reference materials that relate to the study of Chapter 15.

PROCESSES AND CONCEPTS

In conducting this investigation, students may use the following processes:

Observing
Measuring
Inferring
Constructing Models

Using Time/Space
　Relationships
Identifying Variables
Communicating

In conducting this investigation, students may demonstrate knowledge of the following core concepts:

Erosion
Deposition
Stream and river
　sediments

Glaciers and erosion
Glacier valleys
River valleys

TIME NEEDED

The time will vary; one or two class periods should be allowed for the planning and investigation.

PREPARATION

Assemble the materials. Do the activity yourself. This will prepare you to provide assistance to the students during the investigation.

MONITORING THE INVESTIGATION

Tell the students that you want to review and approve their plan before they proceed. Because the steps in the investigation process are linear and sequential, it will be necessary to make any relevant corrections before the plan is put into operation.

After the plan is approved, monitor the work of the students, and respond to their questions and procedural requests. You should not direct their work into any fixed approach. In most performance tasks, there will be different and interesting approaches to solutions.

EXPECTED OUTCOMES

This investigation uses core sample data from different depths to help reconstruct the structure of the layers that underlie a mountain valley. When the students transfer the core data to the work sheet, they will be able to reconstruct the shape of the original valley before it filled with soil. Core sample D is the key to the investigation because it does not show a rounded rock-bedrock interface. This means the depth at the center cannot be determined until more samples are obtained.

Because of this uncertainty, the exact shape of the center of the valley cannot be determined. However, the valley appears to have been V-shaped before it was filled in, thus indicating that a river was involved as an erosion agent at some time. The present U shape of the overall valley, as is given by the topographic map, may lead some students to the conclusion that a glacier may have been active at some time.

Going Further　The current U shape of the valley hints at glacial erosion, while the core samples show the valley had a V shape at one time. This evidence indicates that running water and glaciers may have worked together to shape the valley at different times.

USING THE PERFORMANCE TASK ASSESSMENT LIST

Use the Performance Task Assessment List for Analyzing the Data. Refer to *Performance Assessment in Middle School Science* for a discussion of how to use Performance Task Assessment Lists.

Building for Bugs

Have students complete this performance assessment after they have completed Chapter 16 of the student text. Students should be allowed to use the textbook and any other reference materials that relate to the study of Chapter 16.

PROCESSES AND CONCEPTS

In conducting this investigation, students may use the following processes:

Observing
Measuring
Inferring
Predicting
Using Time/Space
    Relationships

Constructing Models
Identifying Variables
Controlling Variables
Stating Hypotheses
Communicating

In conducting this investigation, students may demonstrate knowledge of the following core concepts:

Populations of organisms
Communities of organisms
Limiting factors
Food chains and food webs
Definition of habitat
Adaptations to limiting factors

TIME NEEDED

The time will vary; two or three class periods should be allowed for the planning and investigation.

PREPARATION

Assemble the materials. Any plastic containers that have screw- or snap-on lids are excellent. Drink bottles, margarine containers, and yogurt containers are examples of containers that can be used.

The diagram shows basic module-construction techniques. An electric drill or a hot nail can be used for making holes for the tubing. If short containers are used, a hole punch might be used. A hot glue gun is very useful if available. You may want to test a few designs before you begin.

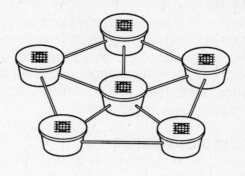

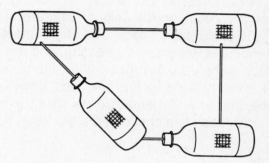

SAFETY

This investigation requires the use of knives and scissors. Warn students to be careful. You may want to supervise the use of the cutting instruments and hot glue gun, if used.

When doing the Going Further section, it must be emphasized that the insects must have adequate food, water, and air supply and must not be otherwise mistreated.

MONITORING THE INVESTIGATION

Be sure that students understand what a *module* is. Many schools may have modular buildings, but even students familiar with the term may use it without really knowing what it means.

Tell the students that you want to review and approve their plan before they proceed. Because the steps in the investigation process are linear and sequential, it will be necessary to make any major corrections before the plan is put into operation.

Building for Bugs (continued)

After the plan is approved, monitor the work of the students, and respond to their questions and procedural requests. You should not direct their work into any fixed approach. In most performance tasks, there will be different and interesting approaches to solutions.

EXPECTED OUTCOMES

This investigation involves all of the concepts and skills necessary to maintain an insect population. It focuses on the unique feature of modular and expandable space. The student designs and modules will prove interesting, and the designs may be very divergent. All of them, however, must provide for life functions, growth space, and environmental factors. Oxygen for the arthropods is a concern. On the other hand, small ants can move through fine mesh or any other hole that is left open. Food and water introduction and waste cycling or removal is another problem. Student designs must address all of these factors.

Going Further This long-term study may be taken on as a class project within the classroom setting. Insect maintenance, habitat modification, and information records can be shared.

USING THE PERFORMANCE TASK ASSESSMENT LIST

Use the Performance Task Assessment List for Model. Refer to *Performance Assessment in Middle School Science* for a discussion of how to use Performance Task Assessment Lists.

Wave Action and Coastlines

Have students complete this performance assessment after they have completed Chapter 17 of the student text. Students should be allowed to use the textbook and any other reference materials that relate to the study of Chapter 17.

PROCESSES AND CONCEPTS

In conducting this investigation, students may use the following processes:

Observing
Measuring
Predicting
Communicating
Constructing Models

Using Time/Space
    Relationships
Identifying Variables
Controlling Variables
Stating Hypotheses

In conducting this investigation, students may demonstrate knowledge of the following core concepts:

Interactions of waves
Properties of waves

Erosion and waves

TIME NEEDED

The time will vary; one to three class periods should be allowed for the planning and investigation.

PREPARATION

Assemble the materials. Construct a shoreline model with gentle slope in the stream table or water container. Use a flat piece of wood or plastic to produce regular, small waves for several minutes. Observe the results. Place a small structure near the water line and repeat the process. This will help you assist the students as they design and conduct their investigations.

MONITORING THE INVESTIGATION

Tell the students that you want to review and approve their plan before they proceed. Because the steps in the investigation process are linear and sequential, it will be necessary to make any relevant corrections before the plan is put into operation.

After the plan is approved, monitor the work of the students, and respond to their questions and procedural requests. You should not direct their work into any fixed approach. In most performance tasks, there will be different and interesting approaches to solutions.

EXPECTED OUTCOMES

This investigation sets up a shoreline model and looks at the effects of wave action on the shoreline and any natural or artificial structures on or near the shoreline. While tidal waves do occur in nature, you should emphasize that the students should use small amplitude, regular frequency waves over a long period of time. Students should practice their wave generating procedures including ways to transfer the wave generator from one student to another. Over long periods of time (30 minutes to one hour) there will be significant changes to the shoreline and structures. These will involve sand bar formation, sand build-up, and slump, erosion, and collapse of structures. Students can attempt to lessen these effects by building groynes (straight structures that are built perpendicular to the shoreline to trap sand), jetties (similar to groynes, but protect harbors and inlets), and seawalls (structures built in front of beaches to prevent waves from reaching them).

Going Further In the Going Further section, students may mention the long-term effects of any structures used to protect shorelines. For example, if a structure lessens erosion by trapping sand, the buildup of sand in a new location may cause different problems. Other factors to consider may include how the structure may interfere with other usage of the shoreline. Is the shoreline used for recreational purposes? Are aquaculture farms present?

USING THE PERFORMANCE TASK ASSESSMENT LIST

You may use one of the following Performance Task Assessment Lists: Model, Making Observations and Inferences, Carrying Out a Strategy and Collecting Data, or Data Table. Refer to *Performance Assessment in Middle School Science* for a discussion of how to use Performance Task Assessment Lists.

Have students complete this performance assessment after they have completed Chapter 18 of the student text. Students should be allowed to use the textbook and any other reference materials that relate to the study of Chapter 18.

PROCESSES AND CONCEPTS
In conducting this investigation, students may use the following processes:

Observing	Using Time/Space Relationships
Measuring	Identifying Variables
Inferring	Controlling Variables
Predicting	Communicating

In conducting this investigation, students may demonstrate knowledge of the following core concepts:

Damage from earthquakes
Constructing buildings to withstand earthquakes
Occurrences of earthquakes
Occurrences of tsunamis
Damage from volcanoes
Occurrences of volcanoes

TIME NEEDED
The time will vary; one or two class periods should be allowed for the planning and investigation.

PREPARATION
Inspect the maps and earthquake and volcano data sheets and analyze the frequency, severity and location of the volcano and earthquake activity. This will help you assist the students when they conduct their investigation.

MONITORING THE INVESTIGATION
Tell the students that you want to review and approve their plan before they proceed. Because the steps in the investigation process are linear and sequential, it will be necessary to make any relevant corrections before the plan is put into operation.

After the plan is approved, monitor the work of the students, and respond to their questions and procedural requests. You should not direct their work into any fixed approach. In most performance tasks, there will be different and interesting approaches to solutions.

EXPECTED OUTCOMES
This investigation involves the effects of volcanoes and earthquakes on human communities. There are several locations on Earth where this occurs. By comparing the frequency and location of the earthquakes and volcanic activity and combining this comparison with the needed requirements for the communities, the students should be able to make and support decisions. The textbook provides excellent background material for this investigation.

For example, a student may choose location C because, although it does not have a sheltered cove for boats, it is farther removed from an active volcano. Either of the other locations might be in danger if Lana Volcano should erupt. Although location A is better protected from earthquake and tsunami damage, most past damage has been on the southeast, not the southwest, coast. Also, Lake Mana and the Mana River would provide a good supply of fresh water to location C. Location C is also far enough away from the fishing village that it will be less likely to destroy the way of life of the people living there.

Remind students that they can approve none, one, two, or all three of the locations. Accept any student responses that the students can justify.

Going Further Other factors to consider may include the impact of a large residential community on the surrounding land and water environment. Consideration should also be given to the culture and historical significance of the area.

USING THE PERFORMANCE TASK ASSESSMENT LIST
You may use one of the following Performance Task Assessment Lists: Analyzing the Data or Data Table.

Earth-Moon Model

Have students complete this performance assessment after they have completed Chapter 19 of the student text. Students should be allowed to use the textbook and any other reference materials that relate to the study of Chapter 19.

PROCESSES AND CONCEPTS

In conducting this investigation, students may use the following processes:

Observing   Constructing Models
Measuring   Identifying Variables
Using Time/Space   Communicating
  Relationships

In conducting this investigation, students may demonstrate knowledge of the following core concepts:

Revolution of Earth   Phases of the moon
Rotation of Earth   Rotation of the moon
Tilt of Earth   Revolution of the
Earth-moon relationships   moon

TIME NEEDED

The time will vary; one to three class periods should be allowed for the planning, investigation, and communication.

PREPARATION

Assemble the materials. The basic model will use the Styrofoam balls attached to the dowel with skewers. You can drill holes in the dowel for the skewers. Be sure the dowel is large enough in diameter that this drilling can be safely done. This method of attachment will be necessary if axis tilt is specified in the design. If you have the facilities, the Styrofoam balls can be painted with Earth and moon colors and fea-

tures. The Earth-Moon Data Tables can be used for reference material.

SAFETY

If students drill holes in the dowel for the skewers, monitor this procedure. A thorough safety briefing should be given before drilling begins.

MONITORING THE INVESTIGATION

Tell the students that you want to review and approve their plan before they proceed. Because the steps in the investigation process are linear and sequential, it will be necessary to make any relevant corrections before the plan is put into operation.

After the plan is approved, monitor the work of the students, and respond to their questions and procedural requests. You should not direct their work into any fixed approach. In most performance tasks, there will be different and interesting approaches to solutions.

EXPECTED OUTCOMES

This investigation involves building a model of the Earth-moon system and using it to demonstrate the phases of the moon, night and day on Earth, eclipses, and tides. It is suggested that the demonstration be oral. Student systems should be such that, when used with a light source, the shadow of Earth on the moon shows phases, the shadow of the moon on Earth shows eclipses, and the light and dark sides of Earth show night and day.

Going Further   Changes in the ocean tides can also be demonstrated using the model.

USING THE PERFORMANCE TASK ASSESSMENT LIST

You may use one of the following Performance Task Assessment Lists: Model or Oral Presentation. Refer to *Performance Assessment in Middle School Science* for a discussion of how to use Performance Task Assessment Lists.

Choosing Plants to Improve the Soil

The Problem

You are working on a beautification project to create a community park. The park will be built on an empty lot that was once the site of a gas station. Before construction can begin, the soil needs to be restored. The soil in some parts of the lot is contaminated with gasoline and oil. In other places, the soil is low in nitrogen, an element needed for plant growth.

A local landscaping company has provided you with information on several different methods that could be used to correct the soil problems. A copy of the landscaper's information appears on the next page. Investigate the matter and use the information given to develop a plan to change the empty lot into a community park.

Materials

paper
markers
metric rulers
field guides and reference
    materials on plants

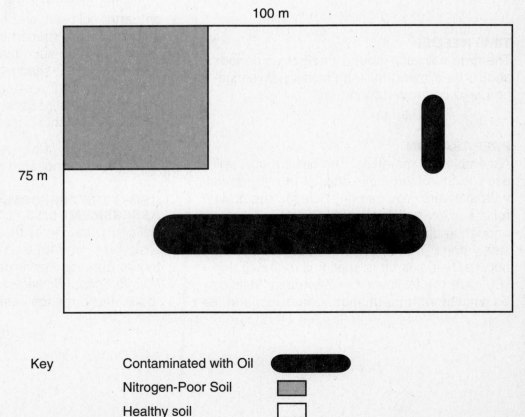

100 m

75 m

Key   Contaminated with Oil

             Nitrogen-Poor Soil

             Healthy soil

Investigation

A. Planning Your Investigation

Study the landscaper's information. Write a plan that explains how you would deal with the contaminated soil. Choose the type of plants you propose to grow. Make a list of the materials you will need and explain how each will be used. Include a projection of how long it will take to convert the lot into a park.

B. Conducting Your Investigation

When you have completed your plan, have it approved by your teacher. Make a scale drawing that shows how the completed park will look. You may change your original plan, if needed, as you work.

C. Communicating Your Results

Summarize the procedure you followed in the investigation and development of your plan. Discuss any changes you made as your plan progressed. Be sure to explain why you selected particular plants for the completed model. Based on the plan you designed, predict how long it will take for the empty lot to be transformed into a park.

Going Further

Discuss how your plan would have differed if you were asked to create a children's playground instead of a park.

Landscapers Information Sheet: Methods of Soil Improvement

Contaminated Soil

Soil contaminated with gasoline and oil is not healthy for plants, animals, or people. Rain may force the gasoline and oil deeper into the soil, allowing chemicals to enter the local water supply through the groundwater. Water runoff can carry oil and gasoline into local rivers, lakes, or streams. Organisms living in these bodies of water may be sickened or killed by the contamination.

Contaminated soil may be removed (dug out) entirely from the area and sent to a processing plant where the oil and gasoline will be removed. New, clean soil may be used to replace the soil, or the old soil, once cleansed, can be returned to the area.

Old soil can be removed and sent to a processing site. A stone garden, concrete surface, sand, or mulch may be used to fill the space once occupied by the soil.

Information About Nitrogen-Poor Soil

Nitrogen-poor soil will not promote healthy plant growth. Nitrogen can be returned to the soil in several ways.

Chemical fertilizers can be used to supply nitrogen to the soil, thus improving the soil fertility. Such chemical treatment needs to be repeated at least four times per year. While chemical fertilizers benefit the soil, they sometimes create problems if they enter water environments.

Plants called legumes help return nitrogen to the soil. Legumes absorb air-borne nitrogen. Bacteria in the plant roots change the nitrogen into a usable form for the legumes. After the legumes die and decay, nitrogen is released into the soil. Soybeans, clover, peas, beans, peanuts, and alfalfa are all legumes.

Using Maps to Choose a Location

The Problem

You are working for a company that wants to build a new manufacturing plant. The new plant will use wood, iron, and plastics to produce several consumer products. The plant can burn oil or coal for the heat needed in its manufacturing process. Its products are fairly small and can be shipped by boat, train, truck, or airplane. The plant will need several thousand gallons of water each day for manufacturing and cooling. After it has been used, this water will be cleaned and cooled before it is returned to the water source. Two different locations, M and X, have been proposed for the plant. You have physical, topographical and natural resource maps for the two areas. Design and carry out an investigation to determine whether the plant should be built at location M or at location X.

Materials

1 ruler
1 United States Map (Appendix G, pp. 642-643, Student Edition)
topographic Map Symbols (Appendix F, p. 641, Student Edition)

Investigation

A. Planning Your Investigation

Plan an investigation that allows you to determine the best location for the manufacturing plant using the physical, topographic, and natural resource maps provided and the other materials furnished. Write a description of the procedure you will follow, and list the materials you plan to use. (You do not have to use all of the materials listed.) Plan a data table to be used in recording your observations.

B. Conducting Your Investigation

When you have completed your plan, and it has been approved by your teacher, conduct the investigation. You may change your original plan, if needed, as you work. Record your observations, and clean up your work station.

C. Communicating Your Results

Summarize the procedure you followed in the investigation, and discuss any changes you made to your plan. Using the results you obtained, state your conclusions about the locations and the reasons for your selection. Draw a map that shows the location of the proposed manufacturing plant based on the results of your investigation.

MAPS

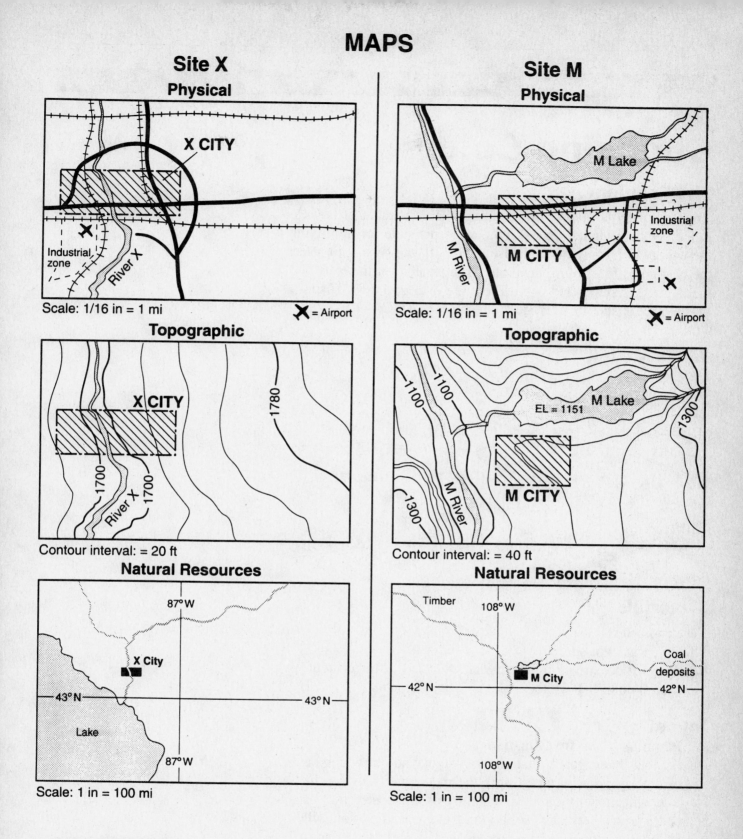

Site X

Physical

X CITY

Industrial zone

River X

Scale: 1/16 in = 1 mi

✈ = Airport

Topographic

X CITY

1780

1700

1700

River X

Contour interval: = 20 ft

Natural Resources

87° W

X City

43° N   43° N

Lake

87° W

Scale: 1 in = 100 mi

Site M

Physical

M Lake

Industrial zone

M River

M CITY

Scale: 1/16 in = 1 mi

✈ = Airport

Topographic

1100

1100

1100

EL = 1151   M Lake

1300

M River

1300

M CITY

Contour interval: = 40 ft

Natural Resources

Timber   108° W

Coal deposits

42° N   M City   42° N

108° W

Scale: 1 in = 100 mi

Going Further

Discuss any other factors that you think should be considered in selecting the best overall site for the plant location. Then draw or build a model of the factory and its surroundings to scale.

Choosing Colors

The Problem

Your company is involved in building a large number of houses in the northern United States. You are responsible for improving the energy efficiency of the houses. One of your jobs is to select the best color for roofing materials. The weather in this part of the country is sunny and cool. There are over 250 days of sunlight per year and the average temperature is 15°C (59°F).

Materials

3 thermometers
1 lamp (heat-light source)
3 squares of construction paper, 8 cm × 8 cm, marked "roof material color" (1 white, 1 black, 1 light brown)

Investigation

A. Planning Your Investigation

Plan an investigation that allows you to find out which color of roofing material will absorb the most heat from the sun. You will model the roof and sun by using construction paper and a lamp. Write a description of the procedure you will follow, and include the materials you plan to use. (You do not have to use all of the materials at the work station.) Plan a data table to be used in recording your observations.

B. Conducting Your Investigation

When you have completed your plan, and it has been approved by your teacher, conduct the investigation. You may change your original plan, if needed, as you work. Record your observations.

After you have conducted the investigation, recorded your observations, and decided on your conclusions, clean up your work station according to your teacher's instructions.

C. Communicating Your Results

Summarize the procedure you followed in the investigation, and discuss any changes you made to your plan. Using the results you obtained, state your conclusions about which color of roofing materials, if any, is best for the northern housing project. Make a chart or graph that shows the results of your investigation.

Going Further

Discuss any other factors that you think should be considered in selecting the overall best color of roofing material for this particular project.

Quieter Cars

The Problem

You are working for a company that manufactures automobiles. Your engineering group leader asks you to conduct a study of how new plastic automobile parts and insulation materials can be used to reduce noise. You are responsible for designing and carrying out an investigation to demonstrate the most effective method for noise reduction.

Materials

1 two-liter plastic drink container with top one-third cut off
1 three-liter plastic drink container section with top one-third cut off
1 sound source (noise-producing clock or timer)
newspaper or paper towels
Styrofoam pieces (cut up drink cups or packing material)

Investigation

A. Planning Your Investigation

Plan an investigation that allows you to find the most effective noise-reduction technique using the materials furnished.

Write a description of the procedure you will follow and the data you will record. Draw a simple diagram of your design, and list the materials you plan to use. (You do not have to use all of the materials at the work station.) Plan a data table to be used in recording your observations.

B. Conducting Your Investigation
When you have completed your plan, and it has been approved by your teacher, conduct the investigation. You may change your original plan, if needed, as you work. Record your observations.

After you have conducted the investigation, recorded your observations, and decided on your conclusions, clean up your work station, and return all the materials to the equipment station.

C. Communicating Your Results
Summarize the procedure you followed in the investigation, and discuss any changes you made to your plan. Using the results you obtained, state your conclusions about the best design for noise reduction using the materials available. Make a diagram, chart, or graph that shows the results of your investigation.

Going Further

Discuss any other factors that you think should be considered in selecting the overall best design for noise reduction.

Automating a Sorting Process

The Problem

Your company mines a mixture that contains three usable raw materials. The three raw materials are solids with different shapes and sizes. At this time, the three solids are separated by hand. You have been asked to develop an automated system that will accurately separate the three usable solids from each other and also from the material that contains them. Use the furnished materials to develop an automated system. Plan and conduct an investigation that demonstrates its operation and how well this automated system works compared to the hand-sorting system now being used.

Materials

4 margarine containers, 48-ounce, or 4 coffee cans
plain white or notebook paper
scissors
1 margarine container lid
1 roll duct tape
1 roll transparent tape
hobby knife
1 cup rice
1 cup peas or small beans
1 cup large beans
2 cups ground coffee
1 can opener
1 measuring cup
1 large container

Investigation

A. Planning Your Investigation

Plan an investigation that allows you to build a system for automating the sorting process. Include a timed experiment that compares sorting time by hand with your system. Write a description of the procedure you will follow and include the materials you plan to use. (You do not have to use all of the materials at the work station.) Plan a data table to be used in recording your observations.

B. Conducting Your Investigation

When you have completed your plan, and it has been approved by your teacher, conduct the investigation. You may change your original plan, if needed, as you work. Record your observations.

After you have conducted the investigation, recorded your observations, and decided on your conclusions, clean up your work station. Return all the reusable materials, and dispose of used tape and paper.

C. Communicating Your Results

Summarize the procedure you followed in the investigation, and discuss any changes you made to your plan. Using the results you obtained, state your conclusions about how the automated system you designed compares to the hand-sorting system. Make a chart or graph that shows the results of your investigation.

Going Further

Discuss any other factors that you think are important about the system you designed and tested.

Reaching High C

The Problem

You work for a laboratory that compares
similar products and compares how
valuable they are to the health of the
people who buy them. At this time, you are
testing similar beverages, comparing the
amounts of vitamin C in each.

You are comparing freshly squeezed orange
juice, orange juice from concentrate, drinks that
have been advertised as containing
"10 percent real orange juice," and
carbonated orange drink. You know
that vitamin C is contained in orange
juice and is an essential factor in resisting
scurvy (see scientific article that follows). You are responsible for
designing and carrying out an experiment to compare the amounts
of vitamin C in several orange drinks.

Materials

100 mL orange juice prepared from concentrate
100 mL freshly squeezed orange juice
100 mL 10 percent orange juice drink
100 mL bottled carbonated orange drink
iodine-starch indicator solution
1 graduated cylinder
1 measuring cup or beaker
1 apron
1 medicine dropper
6 transparent, colorless plastic tumblers
1 metric ruler
1 stirrer

Investigation

A. Planning Your Investigation

Read the two articles, "Vitamin C" and "Testing for Vitamin
C," that follow. Plan an investigation that allows you to
compare the amounts of vitamin C present in each orange
drink. Write a description of the procedure you will follow
and list the materials you plan to use. (You do not have to
use all of the materials at the work station. You may also
request additional materials that your teacher might have on
hand.) Plan a data table for recording your observations.

B. Conducting Your Investigation

When you have completed your plan and it has been approved by your teacher, conduct the investigation. You may change your original plan, if needed, as you work. Record your observations.

After you have conducted the investigation, recorded your observations, and decided on your conclusions, clean up your work station by disposing of all test solutions, cleaning all equipment that was used, and returning all reusable equipment and materials.

C. Communicating Your Results

Summarize the procedure you followed in the investigation, and discuss any changes you made to your plan. Using the results you obtained, state your conclusions about the amount of vitamin C found in the orange juice drinks. Make a diagram, chart or graph that shows the results of your investigation.

Going Further

In performing this test, what did you have to assume to be true about the source of the vitamin C in the drinks? Is this a reasonable assumption or not?

Vitamin C

For several hundred years, sailors, explorers, and other persons in remote and isolated areas had often suffered from a disease called scurvy. Scurvy is caused by a lack of vitamin C in the body. This vitamin was first isolated and identified by a chemist in 1928.

The identification of vitamin C allowed scientists to study its effect in diets. Vitamin C was found to be essential to the health and proper maintenance of blood, bone, and connective tissue. If 60-80 milligrams of vitamin C are not taken in each day, the healthy adult will begin to develop symptoms of scurvy. Over time this can result in death. When vitamin C is restored to the diet, the symptoms of scurvy disappear, and the affected person regains his or her health.

Although they did not know that these foods contain vitamin C, soldiers, sailors, and explorers had found that various foods would combat scurvy. For instance, British sailors were issued limes or lime juice, and this appeared to prevent scurvy. However, when lime or other citrus fruit juices are boiled and processed, much of the vitamin C is destroyed by the heat. Unfortunately, many of the fruits, meats and juices used on ships and other places where fresh food was not readily available were boiled and canned, destroying their value as a source of vitamin C.

Testing for Vitamin C

A blue-colored iodine-starch solution can serve as an indicator for the presence of vitamin C, which is found as a solute in citrus juices. When enough vitamin C is added to a measured amount of the blue indicator, a color change will occur.

The amount of vitamin C present will determine *when* the color change occurs. For example, assume solution A has twice as much vitamin C in it as solution B has. Twice as much solution B would have to be used to bring about the same color change as is seen for a measured amount of solution A.

Acids and Bases in Your Home

The Problem

Your science class has been asked by a citizens'
environmental group to test several common
household products. Your group is to test a
group of soaps, cleaners, and shampoos.
You will use a universal pH indicator to
test whether a solution is acidic, basic, or
neutral. If it is acidic or basic, you will use
its pH to find out how acidic or basic it is.

Materials

6 tumblers
1 graduated cylinder
2 mixing containers
1 bucket or wash basin
rubber gloves
paper towels
water
goggles
apron
universal pH indicator

*Test materials:
  glass cleaner
  standard household cleaner
  scouring cleanser
  bar hand soap
  liquid dishwashing soap
  shampoos
  environmentally safe cleanser
  laundry soap
*assemble 6 to 10 products

Investigation

A. Planning Your Investigation

Plan an investigation that allows you to determine the relative position on the pH scale of the items in the set of test
materials. Write a description of the procedure you will follow and list the materials you plan to use. (You do not have
to use all of the materials at the work station.) Plan a data
table to be used in recording your observations.

B. Conducting Your Investigation

When you have completed your plan, and it has been approved by your teacher, conduct the investigation. You may change your original plan, if needed, as you work. Record your observations.

After you have conducted the investigation, recorded your observations, and decided on your conclusions, clean up your work station and return all reusable materials.

C. Communicating Your Results

Summarize the procedure you followed in the investigation, and discuss any changes you made to your plan. Using the results you obtained, state your conclusions about the pH values of the soaps, shampoos, and cleaners that you tested. Make a diagram, chart, or graph that shows the results of your investigation.

Going Further

Discuss any factors other than those you tested that you think should be considered in the purchase and use of household cleaners, soaps, and shampoos.

Birds of a Feather?

The Problem

You are a technician working in a biological laboratory. A scientist has brought you parts of three bird skeletons found by hunters. The skeleton parts were all found in the same area. There appear to be some differences in size and structure of the birds. You have been asked to study the leg bones of the three skeletons and to classify them based on their similarities and differences.

Materials

bird A leg bones in plastic bag
bird B leg bones in plastic bag
bird C leg bones in plastic bag
hand magnifiers
laboratory balance

paper towels
metric ruler
Optional materials:
  goggles
  electric drill
  small hand saw

Investigation

A. Planning Your Investigation

Plan an investigation that allows you to determine and demonstrate the similarities and differences in the three bird leg bones. Examine the materials and write a description of the procedure you will follow. List the materials you plan to use. (You do not have to use all of the materials at the work station). Plan a data table to be used in recording your observations.

B. Conducting Your Investigation

When you have completed your plan, and it has been approved by your teacher, conduct the investigation. You may change your original plan, if needed, as you work. Record your observations.

After you have conducted the investigation, recorded your observations, and decided on your conclusions, clean up your work station, return all the nondisposable materials to the equipment station, and discard the disposable materials.

C. Communicating Your Results

Summarize the procedure you followed in the investigation, and discuss any changes you made to your plan. Using the results you obtained, state your conclusions about the similarities and differences in the three birds. Make a diagram, chart, or graph that shows the results of your investigation.

Going Further

Conduct similar investigations using fish skeletons or entire bird carcasses.

Rising Expectations

The Problem

You are a scientist working for a food testing laboratory. You want to check the effectiveness of several baker's yeast products. Besides the fact that there are various brands of yeast, is sold in compressed, powdered, and fast-acting forms. Yeast cells are consumers that give off carbon dioxide (CO_2) gas as they consume the sugar in bread dough. Design an experiment to observe and measure the activity of yeast.

Materials

At least two brands of yeast in compressed, powdered, or fast-acting forms, with similar expiration dates.

sugar
balloons
plastic or metal teaspoons
mixing bowl(s)
warm water (250 mL)
graduated cylinder
spoons
metric ruler
thermometer
pencil with eraser
clock
test tubes (22 mm in diameter)
test tube rack
wax marking pencil

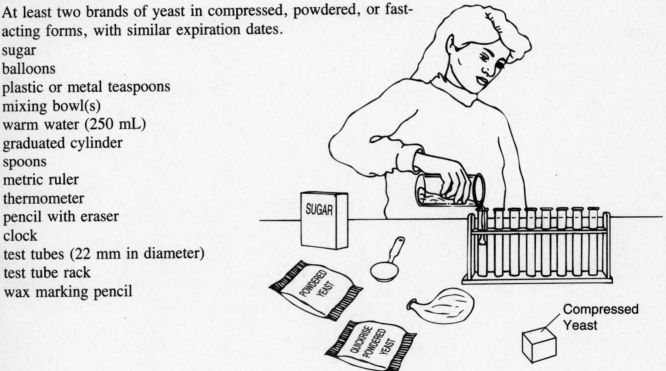

Investigation

A. Planning Your Investigation

Plan an investigation that allows you to determine the quality of each yeast sample. How will you tell whether one brand or form of yeast works better than another? What is the connection between yeast activity and the release of carbon dioxide? How might this be used to measure yeast quality? What variables must be controlled? Write a description of the procedure you will follow. Your plan must state what data you need to evaluate and how you will gather your data. List the materials you plan to use. (You do not have to use all the materials at the work station.) Design a data table in which you will record your observations.

B. Conducting Your Investigation

When you have completed your plan, and it has been approved by your teacher, conduct the investigation. You may change your original plan, if needed, as you work. Record your observations.

After you have conducted the investigation, record your observations. Clean up your work station, return all the non-consumable materials to the equipment station, and discard the disposable materials as directed by your teacher.

C. Communicating Your Results

Study your results, then write a report about the effectiveness of the different brands and forms of yeast. Summarize the procedure you followed in the investigation and discuss any changes you made to your plan. In your report, explain the chemical reaction that occurs between the yeast and the sugar-water solution.

Going Further

Design another experiment to test the effectiveness of various yeast products. This time, use bread dough in the tests. How will you measure the effectiveness of the yeast? What variables need to be controlled? How would you compare the results with those of your first experiment?

Adaptations for Survival

The Problem

You are working for a state government wildlife agency. Your group has been asked to conduct a field survey of an area and locate all the members of two endangered species that were released there four years ago.

Materials

clipboard with paper and pencil
plastic bag

Investigation

A. Planning Your Investigation

Read the Species Identification material on the next page to gather information on the two endangered organisms that were released in the area four years ago. Plan an investigation that will give you current information on how well each of the two species has survived. Write a description of the procedure you will follow.

B. Conducting Your Investigation

When you have completed your plan, and it has been approved by your teacher, conduct the investigation. You may change your original plan, if needed, as you work. Record your observations.

After you have conducted the investigation, recorded your observations, and decided on your conclusions, dispose of any materials that cannot be used again, and return any reusable materials.

C. Communicating Your Results

Summarize the procedure you followed in the investigation, and discuss any changes you made to your plan. Using the results you obtained, state your conclusions about the survival possibilities of the two species. Make a chart or graph that shows the results of your investigation.

Going Further

Discuss how the season in which the investigation is done might affect the results.

Species Identification
History of the Project

Four years ago, two related organisms were reintroduced into the survey area. 20 males and 20 females of *Toothpickus brightus* and 25 males and 25 females of *Toothpickus dullus* were introduced into the area. Both species had been over-hunted during the 1960s and became endangered. A captive-breeding program restored the populations. Four years ago the two related, but differently colored, species were reintroduced into this area.

After a one year period, the area was thoroughly surveyed. It was estimated that 80 percent of the pairs had reproduced. Natural predators such as the *Wolfus pickus* and *Wood bear* were sighted. It is assumed that they have returned to the area to prey on the reintroduced *Toothpickus*.

Due to funding cutbacks, no thorough surveys have been conducted during the past three years. The upcoming survey will be the first opportunity to establish how well each species has reproduced and survived.

Surveying Seed Plants

The Problem

You have been asked to conduct a survey of
seed plants in the area. The local nature
center has prepared an information
sheet about the plants. A copy of
this information sheet is found on
the next page. Use this sheet to
develop a form for your survey.
After your form is complete,
conduct the survey.

Materials

plastic bags
hand magnifier
knife
clipboard
markers
tape
paper clips
metric rulers

Investigation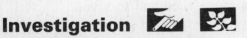

A. Planning Your Investigation

Plan an investigation that allows you to survey the seed
plants in your local area. Depending on your location, sample plants will be furnished, or you will conduct a field survey on your school grounds or in the school neighborhood.
Read the Information Sheet found on the next page, examine
the materials, and write a description of the procedure you
will follow. Construct a seed plant survey form and list the
materials you plan to use. (You do not have to use all of the
materials at the work station). Plan a data table to be used in
recording your observations.

B. Conducting Your Investigation

When you have completed your plan, and it has been approved by your teacher, conduct the investigation. You may
change your original plan, if needed, as you work. Record
your observations.

After you have conducted the investigation, recorded your observations, and decided on your conclusions, clean up your work station, return all the nondisposable materials to the equipment station and discard the disposable materials.

C. Communicating Your Results

Summarize the procedure you followed in the investigation, and discuss any changes you made to your plan. Using the results you obtained, state your conclusions about the number and distribution of seed plants in your survey area. Make a chart or graph that shows the results of your investigation.

Going Further

Discuss any other factors that you think should be considered in surveying the plants in your area.

Information Sheet on Seed Plants

Seed plants are important in our lives. There are about 235,000 known species of seed plants in the world. Seed plants have roots, stems, leaves, and vascular tissue. What makes a seed plant different from simple plants is that it grows from a seed. There are also other differences among seed plants.

Gymnosperms

Gymnosperms are vascular plants that produce seeds on the scales of cones. The word *gymnosperm* comes from the Greek language and means "naked seed." Seeds of gymnosperms are not protected by a fruit. Gymnosperms do not produce flowers. Leaves of most gymnosperms are needlelike or scalelike. Most gymnosperms are evergreen plants that keep their leaves for several years. The gymnosperms include conifers, cycads, ginkgos, and gnetophytes. Conifers are the most common gymnosperms and include pines, firs, cedars, and junipers.

Angiosperms

Angiosperms are vascular plants in which the seed is enclosed inside a fruit. A fruit is a ripened ovary, the part of the plant where seeds are formed. All angiosperms produce flowers. More than half of all known plant species are angiosperms. There are two classes of angiosperms or flowering plants: the monocots and the dicots. The terms *monocot* and *dicot* are shortened forms of the words monocotyledon and dicotyledon. A cotyledon is a seed leaf inside a seed.

Angiosperms—Monocots

Monocots have one seed leaf inside their seeds. Monocots are flowering plants with flower parts appearing in threes or multiples of threes. For example, a flower with six petals would be a monocot. Their vessels are arranged in bundles that are scattered throughout the plant stem. Their leaves have veins that are parallel to each other. Common monocots include cereal grains such as corn, rice, oats and wheat.

Angiosperms—Dicots

Dicots have two seed leaves inside their seeds. Dicots are flowering plants with flower parts in fours or fives. Their vessels are arranged in bundles that appear in rings inside the stem. Their leaves have branching, netlike veins. Examples of dicots include trees like oaks and maples, vegetables like lettuce and beans, fruits like watermelons and oranges, and many garden flowers.

It's Dirty Work

The Problem

You work for a soil analysis laboratory. Your job involves analyzing soil samples for local residents and companies. You have two identical samples from the same location. You can separate the parts of one sample to study its properties. To observe the overall properties of the soil samples, the other sample cannot be broken down, but small amounts of it can be removed for observation and testing. You are to find the water content, composition, color, and depth of horizons for the samples. You also must find out if the samples are acidic or basic and observe any animal or plant life found there.

Materials

2 soil samples, 30-45 cm^3
2 pans or trays
hand magnifiers
probes (skewers, sticks)
set of sieves
laboratory balance
plastic bags
pH paper
plastic sheets (to place under soil samples)
paper towels
table knives (dull)

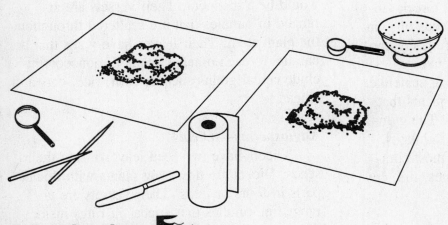

Investigation

A. Planning Your Investigation

Plan an investigation to analyze both soil samples. You can analyze one sample by heating, separating, and sifting. The second sample cannot be destroyed, but it can be observed.

Examine the materials, and write a description of the procedure you will follow. (You do not have to use all of the materials at the work station.) Plan a data table to be used in recording your observations.

B. Conducting Your Investigation

When you have completed your plan, and it has been approved by your teacher, conduct the investigation. You may change your original plan, if needed, as you work. Record your observations.

After you have conducted the investigation, recorded your observations, and decided on your conclusions, clean up your work station, return all the nondisposable materials to the equipment station, and discard the materials that cannot be reused.

C. Communicating Your Results

Summarize the procedure you followed in the investigation, and discuss any changes you made to your plan. Using the results you obtained, state your conclusions about the composition of the soil samples. Make a diagram, chart, or graph that shows the results of your investigation.

Going Further

Discuss any other factors you think should be considered in analyzing the soil sample.

Maximum Motion

The Problem

You are a member of an engineering association that is developing science and engineering activities for middle school students. Your group has been asked to design and build an inexpensive model car that can be used in the classroom to study motion. You are responsible for building a model car and testing it. Your test design should use a ramp to accelerate the car, and the test design goal should be for the model car to travel the maximum distance after being released down the ramp.

Materials

1 stiff cardboard or wooden ramp (25 cm × 90 cm)
1 ruler
1 pencil (sharpened)
4 wheels ("push-up" disks)
2 axles ("push up" sticks)
1 pint milk carton
2 large plastic drinking straws
1 tube or bottle of glue
several metal washers
several books (to elevate ramp)
1 roll tape
1 hobby knife
scissors

Investigation

A. Planning Your Investigation

Plan an investigation that allows you to determine and demonstrate the most efficient design for a gravity-powered model car. Examine the materials and write a description of the procedure you will follow. Draw a simple diagram of the design of your car and the test ramp, and list the materials you plan to use. (You do not have to use all of the materials at the work station). Plan a data table to be used in recording your observations.

B. Conducting Your Investigation

When you have completed your plan, and it has been approved by your teacher, conduct the investigation. You may change your original plan, if needed, as you work. Record your observations.

After you have conducted the investigation, recorded your observations, and decided on your conclusions, clean up your work station, and return all the materials.

C. Communicating Your Results

Summarize the procedure you followed in the investigation, and discuss any changes you made to your plan. Using the results you obtained, state your conclusions about the design of the car and ramp that would give the maximum distance traveled by the car. Make a diagram, chart or graph that shows the results of your investigation.

Going Further

Discuss other materials or features that could be used to improve your overall best design for maximum distance.

Safe Landings

The Problem

You are a college student working for the National Aeronautics and Space Administration (NASA). Your work group has been asked to design a system to safely drop small payloads to the surface of a planet. You are responsible for designing a system that is able to safely land an egg on one flight and a light bulb on another flight. These two payloads represent the delicate instruments that will be used on actual missions.

Materials

plastic drink container, 3 liter
plastic drink container, 2 liter
plastic drink container, 20 ounces
45 cm × 45 cm square of plastic
half-pint milk carton
2 or 3 burned-out light bulbs
styrofoam chips
200 cm kite string
hole punch

paper towels
half-gallon milk carton
1 roll of tape
1 egg
hobby knife
scissors
1 new light bulb
adhesive

Investigation

A. Planning Your Investigation

Plan an investigation that allows you to develop a design for protecting the test payload. You will release your system with the test payload from a height of about 10 meters, and the light bulb must light and the egg must not break in order for your design to be accepted. Write a description of the procedure you will follow, draw a simple diagram of your design, and list the materials you plan to use. (You do not have to use all of the materials at the work station.) Plan a data table to be used in recording your observations.

B. Conducting Your Investigation

When you have completed your plan, and it has been approved by your teacher, conduct the investigation. You may change your original plan, if needed, as you work. Your teacher will furnish you with a burned-out light bulb for design and test purposes. When you are ready to conduct a final test of your system, notify the teacher. The teacher will then authorize you to use the test payloads, which are the egg and the new light bulb. Record your observations during all tests.

After you have conducted the investigation, recorded your observations, and decided on your conclusions, clean up your work station, discard all disposable materials, and return all reusable materials.

C. Communicating Your Results

Summarize the procedure you followed in the investigation, and discuss any changes you made to your plan. Using the results you obtained, state your conclusions about your design for the system that will safely land the payload. Make a diagram, chart or graph that shows the results of your investigation.

Going Further

Compare and contrast a system that would safely land a payload in a near-Earth environment to one that would operate in an environment similar to that of our moon.

Vell, Well, Well

The Problem

You are working in the city planning department for a medium-sized town. The town is expanding and needs a larger water supply. Two locations for wells have been proposed, and your group has been assigned the task of investigating the quality of the water from each of the two locations. To do this, you will use models of the layers of soil and rock for the two drainage areas and analyze the runoff to decide which location would produce the higher quality water for the new water supply.

Materials

2 soil-rock column models
2 graduated cylinders
1 laboratory balance
2 beakers
filter paper
pH paper
2 hand magnifiers
2 funnels

Investigation

A. Planning Your Investigation

Plan an investigation that allows you to find and demonstrate the quality of water samples from models of two different soil-rock layer combinations. Examine the materials and write a description of the procedure you will follow. List the materials you plan to use. (You do not have to use all of the materials at the work station.) Plan a data table to be used in recording your observations.

B. Conducting Your Investigation

When you have completed your plan, and it has been approved by your teacher, conduct the investigation. You may change your original plan, if needed, as you work. Record your observations.

After you have conducted the investigation, recorded your observations, and decided on your conclusions, clean up your work station, dispose of the used paper, and return all other materials.

C. Communicating Your Results

Summarize the procedure you followed in the investigation, and discuss any changes you made to your plan. Using the results you obtained, state your conclusions about the water quality of the samples from the two different soil-rock column models. Make a diagram, chart or graph that shows the results of your investigation.

Going Further

Discuss any other factors that you think should be considered in selecting the best location for a new city water supply.

own in the Valley

he Problem

You are working for a geological survey party that is mapping the structure of a mountain valley. The survey party has drilled a series of holes across the valley to a depth of fifty feet in order to collect soil and rock samples. Your task is to use the maps, diagrams, and core sample data to determine what caused the erosion that shaped the valley.

Materials

1 ruler

Investigation

A. Planning Your Investigation

Plan an investigation that allows you to determine the structure of the layers that underlie the mountain valley. Examine the figure on this page, the Core Data Sheet, and the Survey Work Sheets, and write a description of the procedure you will follow.

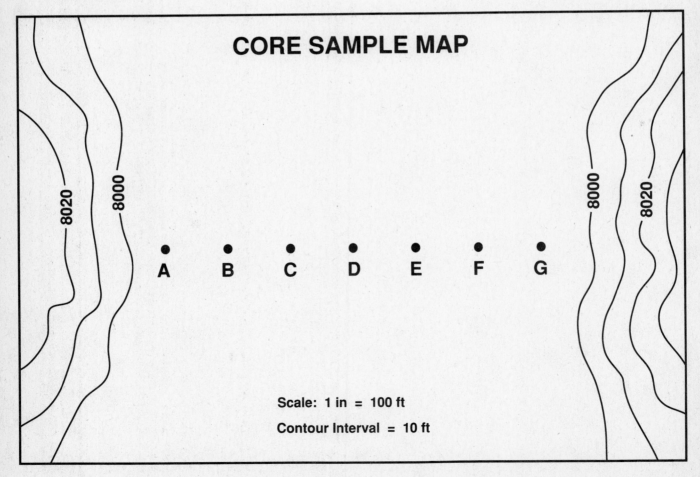

CORE SAMPLE MAP

8020 8000   •   •   •   •   •   •   •   8000 8020
                    A   B   C   D   E   F   G

Scale: 1 in = 100 ft

Contour Interval = 10 ft

B. Conducting Your Investigation

When you have completed your plan, and it has been approved by your teacher, conduct the investigation. You may change your original plan, if needed, as you work. Record your observations on one of the Survey Work Sheets.

After you have conducted the investigation, recorded your observations, and decided on your conclusions, clean up your work station, and return the ruler to the equipment station.

C. Communicating Your Results

When you are satisfied with your work, transfer your results to the second Survey Work Sheet. Next, summarize the procedure you followed in the investigation and discuss any changes you made to your plan. Finally, using the results you obtained, state your conclusions about the structure of the valley and what caused the erosion.

Going Further

Discuss any evidence you have discovered that indicates that several factors worked together to shape the valley.

CORE DATA SHEET

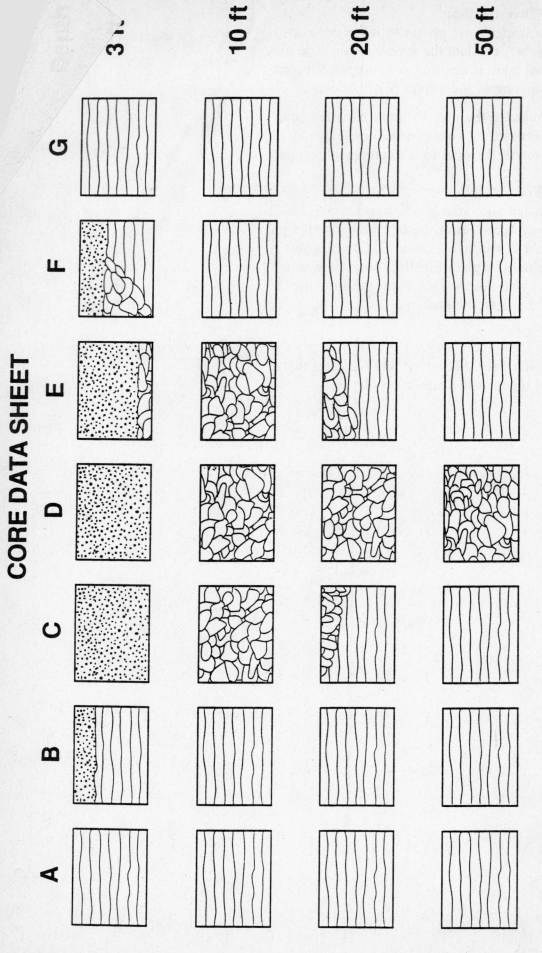

KEY:

Sandy soil

Rounded rocks

Unweathered bedrock

SURVEY WORK SHEET

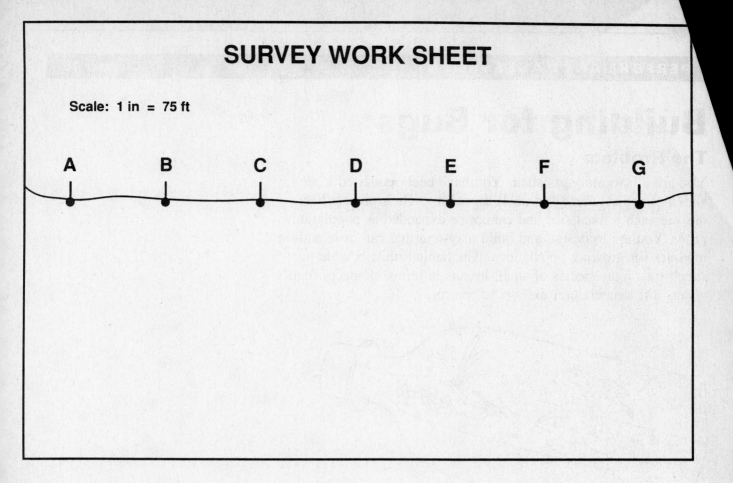

Scale: 1 in = 75 ft

A   B   C   D   E   F   G

SURVEY WORK SHEET

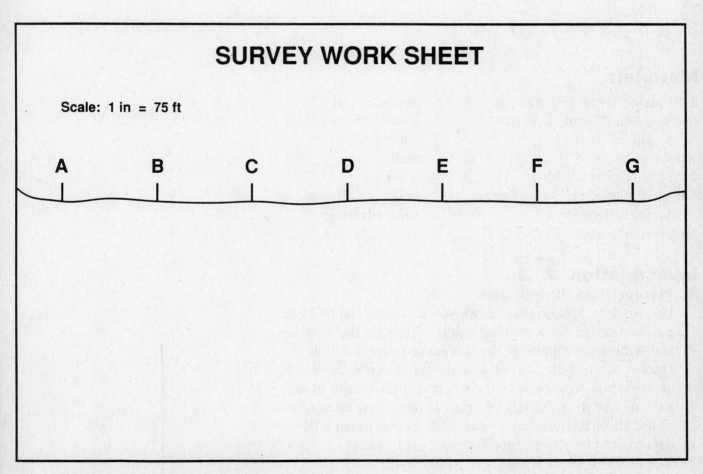

Scale: 1 in = 75 ft

A   B   C   D   E   F   G

uilding for Bugs

e Problem

You are a laboratory assistant. You have been requested to design a modular habitat for small organisms. Their present habitats are each a fixed size and cannot be expanded as populations grow. You are to design and build a system that can have add-on modules for growing populations. The habitat must be able to support a single species of small insects in terms of space, food, water, air, temperature, and waste control.

Materials

8-10 plastic containers with lids
nylon screen (30 cm × 30 cm)
hobby knives
scissors
2 meters of plastic tubing
4-6 small plastic or
    styrofoam containers
plug material (cork, clay)

medicine vial lids
1 tube silicon adhesive
potting soil
sand
water
twigs
small plants
1 roll tape

Investigation

A. Planning Your Investigation

Plan an investigation that allows you to design and build an efficient design for a modular habitat. Examine the materials and write a description of the procedure you will follow. Draw a detailed diagram of your design; describe the use of each module and how it will connect and disconnect to the habitat. List the materials you plan to use. (You do not have to use all of the materials at the work station.) Plan a design data log to be used in recording your observations.

B. Conducting Your Investigation

When you have completed your plan, and it has been approved by your teacher, conduct the investigation. You may change your original plan, if needed, as you work. Record your observations.

After you have conducted the investigation, recorded your observations, and decided on your conclusions, clean up your work station, discard all disposable materials, and return all reusable materials.

C. Communicating Your Results

Summarize the procedure you followed in the investigation, and discuss any changes you made to your plan. Using the results you obtained, state your conclusions about the best design for modular insect habitats. Make a diagram that shows the results of your investigation.

Going Further

If possible, select a specific insect species, place it into the habitat, and undertake a long-term study that includes several natural cycles of the organism. Maintain a log and modify your habitat as needed. Be certain that insects are properly cared for.

ave Action and Coastlines

he Problem

You are working at a university on a project on coastal erosion.
Your group is modeling the effect of wave action on shorelines.
You have been asked to set up a system to produce wave action
on a model coastline and study the effects of these waves on the
shoreline. Then, submit ideas for lessening coastal erosion.

Materials

1 stream table or similar container
1 plastic or plywood wave generator
several wood or plastic blocks
small pebbles, stones, and rocks
other model construction materials
sand
water

Investigation

A. Planning Your Investigation

Plan an investigation that allows you to create wave action
on a shoreline and study its effect. Then plan how any
coastal erosion could be lessened. Examine the materials and
experiment with the stream table, sand, water, and wave

generator until you can create small waves on a model shore-line. Draw a simple diagram of your proposed experiment and list the materials you plan to use. (You do not have to use all of the materials at the work station). Plan a data table to be used in recording your observations.

B. Conducting Your Investigation

When you have completed your plan, and it has been approved by your teacher, conduct the investigation. You may change your original plan, if needed, as you work. Record your observations.

After you have conducted the investigation, recorded your observations, and decided on your conclusions, clean up your work station and return all the nondisposable materials to the equipment station.

C. Communicating Your Results

Summarize the procedure you followed in the investigation, and discuss any changes you made to your plan. Using the results you obtained, state your best design for protecting shorelines from wave action.

Going Further

Discuss any other factors that you think should be considered in selecting the best design for shoreline protection.

Build or Not to Build

e Problem

ou are a member of a planning committee for a group of islands in the Pacific Ocean. A resort development company has applied for a permit to build a large residential community on Mana Lana Island. At this time there is only one small fishing village on the north coast of the island. This project would bring 10 to 20 times the number of people and buildings to the island as are there now. Each of the three proposed locations would include a golf course, boating storage and docks, hotels and condominiums, and houses. The development company has shown by numbers on their map which building locations they like best. Your committee's job is to study the maps and historical data that follow, including volcano and earthquake activity, and make a decision. You can approve all of the locations, two, one, or none of the locations. Your decision is final.

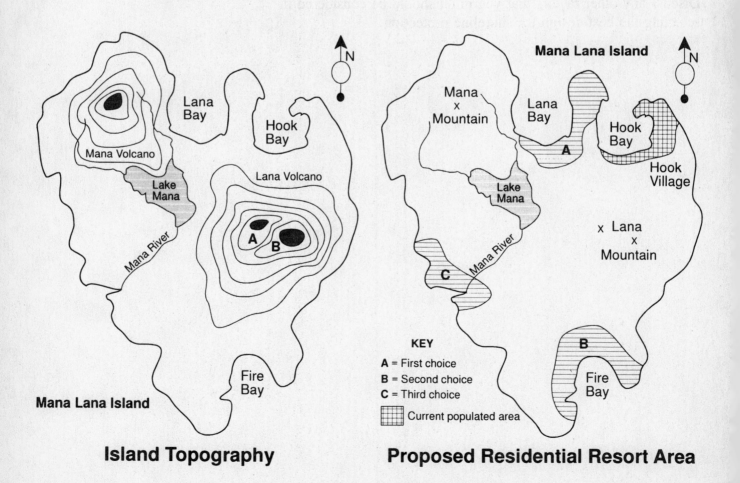

KEY

A = First choice
B = Second choice
C = Third choice
Current populated area

Island Topography   **Proposed Residential Resort Area**

Investigation

A. Planning Your Investigation

Plan an investigation that uses the data on the maps and data sheets to help you decide where and if a large resort community could be located on the island. Write a description of the procedure you will follow. Plan a data table to be used in recording your observations.

B. Conducting Your Investigation

When you have completed your plan, and it has been approved by your teacher, conduct the investigation. You may change your original plan, if needed, as you work. Record your observations.

After you have conducted the investigation, recorded your observations, and decided on your conclusions, clean up your work station.

C. Communicating Your Results

Summarize the procedure you followed in the investigation, and discuss any changes you made to your plan. Using the results you obtained, state your conclusions for the best location for the resort location. Make a chart or graph that shows the results of your investigation.

Going Further

Discuss any other factors that you think should be considered in selecting the best location for the resort location.

na Island
cano

	LOCATION	DURATION	COMMENTS
/	Main Vent	4 days	lava flow east
.764	Main Vent	6 days	lava flow east
1790	Main Vent	1 day	no lava flow
1847	Main Vent	2 days	no lava flow

Lana Volcano

YEAR	LOCATION	DURATION	COMMENTS
1737	Vent A	2 days	lava flow north
1790	Vent A	10 days	lava flow north
1847	Vent A	6 days	lava flow north
1847	Vent B	4 days	lava flow south
1903	Vent A	11 days	lava flow north
1903	Vent B	7 days	lava flow south
1943	Vent A	2 days	no lava flow
1943	Vent B	2 days	lava flow south

Mana Volcano was very active until the 19th century when its intensity decreased. It has had no significant activity during the current century.

Lana Volcano is active. With the opening of a second vent (Vent B) in 1847, lava has flowed both north and south.

Significant Earthquake Data She

Mana Lana Island

The Rim of Fire Fault Line is located south of
Mana Lana Island. This is a major earthquake
activity area that produces significant earthquakes and, on occasion, tsunamis that radiate
from a point on the fault line.

YEAR	MAGNITUDE	COMMENTS
1814	8.3	No deaths reported
1885	unknown	6 deaths; tsunami destroyed southeast coast
1905	5.3	No significant damage
1921	4.9	No significant damage
1939	6.3	8 deaths; significant structural damage
1963	7.1	11 deaths; significant coastal damage
1989	6.5	3 deaths; tsunami hit southeast coast

th-Moon Model

Problem

ou have been asked to design and build a model of the Earth-moon system. The model should be capable of demonstrating the relative motion of Earth and the moon. The system does not have to be a scale model. With a light source as a model of the sun, you should be able to show the cause and effect relationships that produce day and night on Earth, the phases of the moon, eclipses, and tides.

Materials

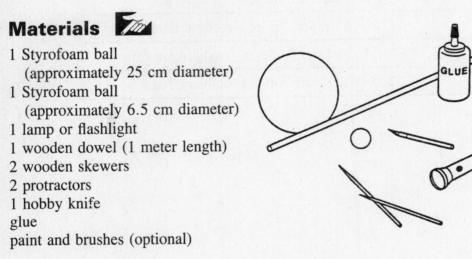

1 Styrofoam ball
   (approximately 25 cm diameter)
1 Styrofoam ball
   (approximately 6.5 cm diameter)
1 lamp or flashlight
1 wooden dowel (1 meter length)
2 wooden skewers
2 protractors
1 hobby knife
glue
paint and brushes (optional)

Investigation

A. Planning Your Investigation

Plan an investigation to design and construct an Earth-moon system model. The model should be capable of being used to show the phases of the moon and other Earth-moon interactions. Examine the materials and write a description of the procedure you will follow. Draw a diagram of your design and list the materials you plan to use. (You do not have to use all of the materials at the work station).

B. Conducting Your Investigation

When you have completed your plan, and it has been approved by your teacher, conduct the investigation. You may change your original plan, if needed, as you work. Record your observations.

After you have conducted the investigation, recorded your observations, and decided on your conclusions, clean up your work station, and return all the materials to the equipment station.

C. Communicating Your Results

Make a presentation that shows the results of your investigation. Use your model to help explain how day and night, phases of the moon, eclipses, and tides occur. State your conclusions about the best design for the Earth-moon system.

Going Further

Discuss any other relationships that you can demonstrate with the Earth-Moon system model.

Earth-Moon Data Tables

Earth

Revolution around sun	365 days
Orbital speed	30 km/sec
Distance from sun	149,600,000 km
Rotation	23 hrs 56 min.
Axis tilt	23.45°
Diameter	12,756 km

Moon

Revolution around Earth	27.3 days
Orbital speed	1.026 km/sec
Distance from Earth	384,400 km
Rotation	27.3 days
Axis tilt	6.68°
Diameter	3,476 km